the yarn lover's guide to
hand dyeing

Silk on the shelf at Treenway Silks (page 95).

the yarn lover's guide to
hand dyeing

BEAUTIFUL COLOR AND SIMPLE KNITS

LINDA LA BELLE

Photography by

Donna Alberico • Kristin Duvall • Linda LaBelle

POTTER CRAFT

New York

Published in the United States by Potter Craft,
an imprint of the Crown Publishing Group,
a division of Random House, Inc., New York.
www.crownpublishing.com
www.pottercraft.com

POTTER CRAFT and CLARKSON N. POTTER
are trademarks, and POTTER and colophon are
registered trademarks of Random House, Inc.

The following patterns were used by permission.
Ruffled Baby Socks pattern on page 36 copyright © Darlene Hayes. Used with permission.
Feather Lace Hat pattern on page 42 copyright © Kimberly Kauffman. Used with permission.
Lace Gauntlets pattern on page 48 copyright © Lori Lawson. Used with permission.

Grateful acknowledgment is made to Jen Fong
Photography for permission to reprint one photograph
of an Icelandic sheep by Jen Fong. Reprinted by
permission of Jen Fong Photography.

All other photographs are new by Linda LaBelle,
Donna Alberico, and Kristin Duvall

Library of Congress Cataloging-in-Publication Data
LaBelle, Linda.
    The yarn lovers guide to hand dyeing : beautiful
color and simple knits / by Linda LaBelle ;
photography by Donna Alberico, Kristin Duvall,
Linda LaBelle. — 1st ed.
        p.   cm.
    Includes index.
    ISBN 978-0-307-35253-8
1. Dyes and dyeing, Domestic.   2. Dyes and dyeing—
Textile fibers.   3. Knitting.   I. Title.
TT853.L32   2007
746.6'041—dc22   2007009382

Printed in China

Design by Chalkley Calderwood

10 9 8 7 6 5 4 3 2 1

First Edition

For mb—if not for the seed you planted,
The Yarn Tree wouldn't be!

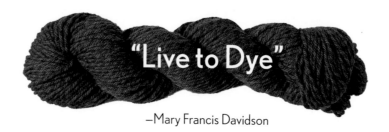

"Live to Dye"

—Mary Francis Davidson

contents

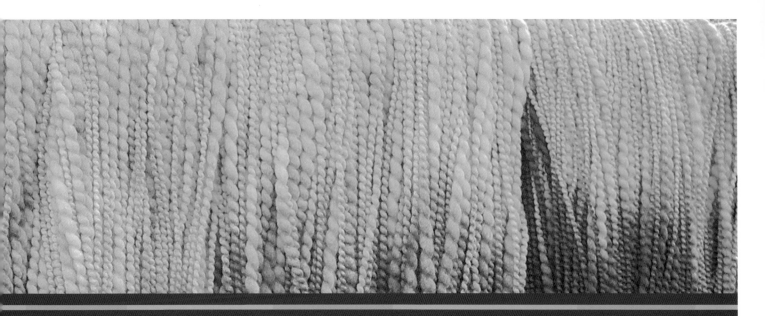

introduction

The idea for a book on dyeing was inspired by Shawna Mullen of Potter Craft. What is inside the covers of this book originates from The Yarn Tree and a community of very talented people. Knitters are beginning to want to do more than just knit! They want to explore the world beyond their needles by learning to spin their own yarn and create their own colors. My customers and students are always asking me, "How can I dye at home?" The answer is in this book. This book celebrates color and shows how you can easily bring a little color into your creative life. With clear instructions, fun projects, and lots of how-to tips, this is a book that will be of interest to the novice as well as the experienced crafter.

In addition to dye recipes and how-tos (there is even a chapter on dyeing with Kool-Aid and food coloring that you can do with your kids!), you will find knitting and crochet patterns from The Yarn Tree and, best of all, if you don't want to dye the yarn yourself, we've provided alternative manufacturers' yarns for you to knit with.

We also celebrate some of the wonderful hand dyers around the country, through interviews and photographs. You'll get a behind-the-scenes look at their studios, see how their environment affects their color sense, and follow threads that link them to each other.

This book is really a collaboration—every customer who has walked through the doors of my shop, every student who has sat around our tables or worked in our studio has had a hand in shaping this book.

For example, Chapter 3 on Ashford Wool Dyes (using the cold pad method) is in the book because one of my customers, Rachel DeNys, needed a way to dye the white gloves she knit for her wedding. She wanted to continue to wear them, but wanted them to be a color, and she couldn't afford any shrinkage. I realized she wasn't the only knitter who wished to dye something after it had been knit.

Another project stemming out of customer concerns was the overdyeing of previously colored yarn. Too often I've overheard someone say, "I really like the yarn, but I wish it were another color," or "I wish it were variegated." Here we've solved that dilemma for you! We will show you which dyes are suitable to use on an already dyed manufacturer's yarn. Think: hot pink yarn, but you wish it had some black accents—not hard to do—or 10 skeins of yellow wool purchased on sale that seemed like a great idea at the time, but you'd rather they were any other color—easy to accomplish.

Here is a bit of advice—don't be afraid to make mistakes.

Experiment, try out your ideas. Mistakes are an opportunity for learning! Often it is the "mistake" that takes you down the creative path. If the dyers I interviewed had been afraid to make mistakes, their businesses would never have come into existence!

Come along with me as I take you on a dyer's journey from The Yarn Tree's dye room to the neighbor's kitchen, from the backyard to the studio.

a brief overview

The following chapter will help to give you a general idea of what is required for hand dyeing at home. Safety, tools, dyes, and techniques are covered.

Mary Paddon takes precautions when working in her studio. While wearing rubber gloves and a respirator, she adds acetic acid to the dyepot.

Safety in Dyeing

Dyeing yarn and fiber is a very exciting experience, but one that requires some caution and protective measures.

All utensils used for dyeing should be just that—*only* used for dyeing.

If the expense of buying all new pots, measuring cups, etc puts you off, go to thrift stores or garage sales. In my neighborhood in Brooklyn we have discount stores, and this is where I shop for my enamel pots.

When you measure out the dye powder, *do not* do it near food or eating utensils.

Cover the area where you are measuring out the dye with newspaper, be sure to stay clear of any breezes, wear a dust mask and gloves, and carefully place the dye powder in the container and then turn it into a paste with a small amount of warm water. Once in paste form, it is a much safer product. Always keep the containers closed when not in use!

Why do you have to wear a dust mask and gloves? Because the dye powder is very fine, and you don't want to breathe it, nor do you want it getting on your skin. I use nitrile gloves to protect my skin.

Once you develop a sensitivity to chemical dyes, unfortunately that sensitivity will compound, so each time you use the dyes you will become a little more sensitive. The end result is that there could be a time when you would no longer be able to work with the dyes. A little precaution means you can enjoy this craft for a very long time.

A question I am often asked is, "Do you need to neutralize the dyebath when you are ready to pour the liquid down the drain?" The majority of the time, your dyebath will be exhausted of color, and you can pour the liquid right down the drain. The pH of most dyebaths is around 6.5—close to tap water—so I don't feel that it is necessary to neutralize the dyebath. But if the dyebath hasn't exhausted and you want to neutralize the liquid in the pot, you can add a pinch of baking soda or soda ash.

Color Theory

This is a most basic introduction to color theory. There are many books and online tutorials that are readily available. A very helpful book on color theory is the book *Colorworks: the Crafter's Guide to Color,* by Deb Menz.

Do you remember Roy G. Biv from grade school? Well, the letters stand for Red, Orange, Yellow, Green, Blue, Indigo, and Violet.

The Color Wheel

First there are the primary colors: red, yellow, and blue.

If you mix equal amounts of two primary colors you will get a secondary color:

Red + Blue = Violet

Red + Yellow = Orange

Blue + Yellow = Green

The secondary colors sit opposite the primary colors on the color wheel.

Blue—Orange

Red—Green

Yellow—Violet

If you mix a primary color and a secondary color, you will get a tertiary color. The tertiary colors are yellow-orange, red-orange, red-violet, blue-violet, blue-green, and yellow-green.

You do need to be careful when mixing primary and secondary colors! Yes, red and orange make red-orange, but red and green make a muddy brown. Blue and violet make blue-violet, but blue and orange make gray, as do yellow and violet.

If I want to tone down a color—say my red is just too bright—then I will add a drop of its complementary color—green—but just a drop!

For richer colors, I will dye a light silver or fawn-colored yarn. For intense bright color, I use white yarn.

When I paint yarn, I choose my dominant color—this is what you will see the most of. The painted area will be longer or wider or occur more often than any of the other colors. Then comes the second most dominant, then the third, and so on.

As I am painting, I am very careful to leave space between my colors, because the dye will spread during the setting process. Also, I'm careful about what colors may touch each other. I may want to have blue next to orange, but I know if they touch the result will be a muddy color, so I am sure to leave white space, then when the dye does spread the blending of the two is minimal.

The key to a successfully handpainted yarn is to keep your colors clean and be aware of what sits next to each other—so take your time to plan out where your colors will sit on the skein. You don't want to go to all this trouble and effort to end up with mud!

The Tools

The tools needed for dyeing are fairly basic. What is important about them is that you keep them separate from your cooking utensils. *Never* use the same pot to dye in and later make spaghetti sauce. The dyes are nontoxic when used properly; it is simply good studio practice to separate your studio equipment from equipment used for food preparation.

Kool-Aid contains a food colorant that acts as an acid dye when vinegar is added, so when dyeing with Kool-Aid and food coloring you do not need separate equipment.

Here is a list of materials that will make your dyeing adventures most successful.

The pots must be enamel or stainless steel, not aluminum or cast iron. The reason for this is that both aluminum and cast iron can affect your color. The pots must be large enough that when you are doing immersion dyeing the yarn can move freely in the pot.

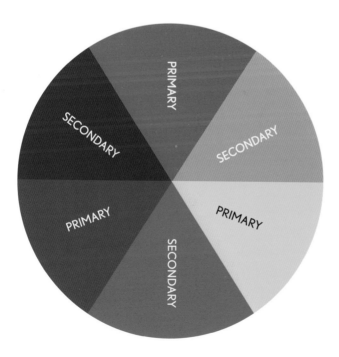

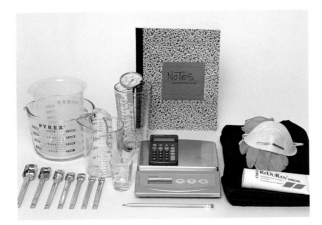

The Tools

- Notebook
- Scale (one that can weigh grams as well as ounces)
- Measuring spoons (stainless steel or plastic)
- Glass and plastic measuring cups (American measure & metric)
- Calculator
- Apron
- Protective gloves (I use nitrile gloves)
- Dust mask (disposable)
- Reduran (for getting dye off your hands)
- Candy thermometer
- Enamel Pots (various sizes)
- Vegetable steamer (metal)
- Microwavable bowl
- Large spoons (plastic ladles)
- Clear plastic cups
- 12" ruler
- Acrylic yarn, 1 skein
- Basin for rinsing
- Drying rack
- Timer
- Pot holders
- Mason jars (wide mouth, various sizes)
- Masking tape
- Waterproof marker
- Heavy-duty, resealable plastic containers
- Metal muffin tin
- 1" and 2" foam brushes
- Syringes (plastic)
- Small metal whisk
- Measuring tape
- Niddy noddy
- Plastic wrap
- Paper towels
- Newspaper
- Plastic sheeting (or large trash bags)
- Skeining tool

I mentioned earlier that I get my enamel pots from a discount store in my neighborhood. Go to thrift stores and yard sales to find some for yourself. Look for used enamel pots that are not chipped. Under the enamel is iron, so if the pot is chipped the iron will leech into the dyebath and gray down (sadden) your color. You can use this to your advantage, though: I have a particular pot I use when I'm dyeing with natural dyes and I want to obtain a certain shade of green. The pot has a quarter-size chip in the enamel, and just enough iron leeches into the dyebath to sadden my green and give me the color I desire!

You will need large ladles—I prefer to use plastic versus wood because the plastic spoons clean up more easily than wooden ones.

My preference in measuring spoons is stainless steel because they don't stain, but these are expensive, and plastic ones are fine.

For glass measuring cups, I like the four-cup (1L) size. Look for ones that measure in both American standard and metric. I have a variety of shapes and sizes, one of my favorites is the Liquid Measure from The Baker's Catalogue. It is perfect for measuring out small amounts of liquid. It measures in teaspoons, tablespoons, ounces, and milliliters!

I use a digital scale that can measure in both ounces and grams with precision.

A disposable dust mask is good to have when measuring out any powdered dyes. The dye powder is very, very fine, and you want to avoid inhaling it!

I use disposable nitrile gloves when working with the dyes and regular kitchen gloves when I am lifting yarn out of the soak solution or rinsing the yarn. A great tip came from Cheryl Huseby Wiebe and Mary Paddon (Treenway Silks dyers, page 95)—always buy your kitchen gloves one size larger than you need, because then they are much easier to slip on and off!

I always keep one or two skeins of acrylic on hand as this has many uses, for tying figure 8s, larkshead knots, or a nice big loop through the skein to make it easier to lift the skein in and out of the pot. Also, if I've run out of yarn while making a long skein, I will tie on acrylic yarn and continue back to the beginning to complete the skein and tie it off.

Metal muffin tins are the perfect tool to hold your small containers of dyestock. I find the aluminum foil ones are a little too flimsy, so if these are all you can find, be sure to double them up.

Dyestock is poured into wide-mouth Mason jars so individual sections of a skein can be dyed. See page 78 to learn this multicolored soak technique.

The Dyes

When I began the research for this book, I ordered many different manufacturers' dyes. Some didn't make it into the book—merely a matter of space. If you don't see a dye used here, it doesn't mean you shouldn't try it out!

There are many brands of acid dyes. They all work in basically the same manner (heat, acid, and time), but the major difference is the palette. Each manufacturer has its own color palette.

All of these dyes are available through my shop and at art supply stores, craft stores, some yarn shops, as well as online. I looked for easy-to-use dyes and dyes that came in kit form.

I tested a variety of thickeners (used to slow down or stop the bleeding of the dyes). If you want, you could probably choose one and use that throughout—they each give a different effect, though. The gum tragacanth is very thick and can stop bleeding in its tracks, while Jacquard Superclear is less thick and will allow for a little bleed. Any thickener can be thinned down by adding a little warm water until it reaches the desired consistency. I recommend that you

do some experimentation and see what works for you.

As for the acids—I worked with either citric acid or distilled white vinegar; you could pick one. To substitute distilled white vinegar for citric acid: 1 tbsp (15mL) citric acid = 11 tbsp (165mL) distilled white vinegar.

Note that the water where you live can affect the dye. Soft water is not a problem. If you have hard water, you can soften it with Metaphos or Calgon. You can also use distilled water, usually available through your grocery store or pharmacy. To find out if you have hard water, you can take a sample to your local health department and get it tested.

All of the dyers I interviewed mentioned that one should be aware of how dyes can change. What you buy today may not be exactly the same when you get a new batch six months from now. The color could be slightly different, it could be more or less granular, the ph level or mineral content of the water might change, or the humidity can be different—all of these variables will affect your color. The dyer must be flexible when Murphy's Law prevails!

The Techniques

I originally trained as a fine artist, and to this day I find nothing more exciting than touching a brush to canvas. In this case my canvas is yarn made from natural fibers!

My methods are labor intensive, but I never imagined this as a book for the production dyer (a person who is dyeing many pounds of yarn per day for resale).

The techniques defined:

Immersion This involves adding dye and any assistants (acids or other chemicals) to a pot with enough water to cover the yarn—then add your presoaked yarn. This process requires heat and time. Immersion can be accomplished with both protein and cellulosic yarns or fibers.

Faux Ikat This is a method of wrapping the yarns with plastic wrap prior to dyeing—the wrapped areas will not absorb color. You then immersion-dye the yarn.

Cold Pad This is a method of dyeing without heat—the painted yarn is wrapped in plastic and allowed to cure at 75–80°F (24–27°C) for a minimum of 24 hours. Cold Pad works with both protein and cellulosic yarns or fibers.

Syringe/Microwave This is a method where you can quickly add color to yarn using water, vinegar, acid dyes, and a syringe and set the color in a microwave. Recommended for protein yarn or fibers only.

Soak The yarn is soaked in jars of dyestock made from acid dyes with the necessary assistants added. After 15 minutes or so, the yarn is removed, then wrapped in plastic wrap and steamed. Recommended for protein yarn or fibers only.

Handpaint A dyestock is mixed up and the necessary assistants are added. The yarn is literally painted by hand. If you are working on protein fibers, the end result needs to be steamed. If you are working on cellulosic fibers, the end result is wrapped in plastic and left to cure at 75–80°F (24–27°C) for a minimum of 24 hours.

The Skeins

You will notice that for many of the techniques I used very long skeins. You might be saying, "Okay, but how can I do that?" Well, there are several ways. While testing out the techniques, I designed a skeining tool that makes very long skeins, and you can buy it through my shop or website. But there are other options. Often purchased yarn will be in a skein, but these skeins sometimes are not long enough or are too dense for our purposes. You will need to ball up these skeins and then make the balls into long skeins.

To make the skeins into balls, you can stretch the skein over a swift and then wind by hand or onto a ball winder. Or stretch it on the skeining tool, someone's outstretched arms, or the back of a chair—the only important thing is that the skein be under tension.

Once you have the ball complete, you can make any size skein. Without a skeining tool, you can place two chairs as far apart as needed and then wind the yarn around their backs, or you can turn two tables upside down, placing them as far apart as needed, and wind the yarn around one leg of each of the tables. For shorter skeins, you can use a niddy noddy. Once you have your skein made, and before you remove it from tension, you need to keep the yarn under control by making at least four figure 8 ties around the skein using acrylic yarn (the acrylic will not take up the dye).

Handpainting is a method of applying color to your yarn. Learn how to make this confetti yarn on page 104.

Why do I work with such long skeins? The longer skeins will allow you to get better color distribution, lessening the likelihood of color pooling. I think the results are obvious in the pictures of the finished garments

These techniques should be a stepping off point for you. Try them, learn from them, and then let your imagination take over. All of the dyers I interviewed echoed the same thing—don't be afraid to experiment!

The Interviews

I would have to say the most exciting part of writing this book was the opportunity to interview some of the hand dyers whom I admire. The first interview was a car ride away in the Finger Lakes region of New York state, while the final interview would take me across the country to Victoria Island, BC, where I would hop a ferry to Salt Spring Island. There I would be visiting three studios, Treenway Silks, owned by Karen Selk and Terry Nelson, and the studios of two of the women who dye for Treenway.

I didn't think about gender until someone asked me why I had chosen only women to interview. It wasn't intentional. I wasn't thinking of the person behind the beautiful yarns and fiber as male or female, only as an artist that I wanted to know better.

It was important to me to shoot in as much natural light as possible, although the camera did have a flash. Nothing was ever staged or styled. I did find out as the interviews progressed that each of the dyers was a little nervous about my visit, and everyone cleaned up their studios.

When I started out, I had no idea of the threads I would find that tie these women together. Several of them knew each other personally, others knew of each other, others were strangers. Love of what they do, the excitement of color, and the magical touch of fiber is the strongest thread that links them. Their eyes light up when they talk about how good it makes them feel at the end of the day to see the yarns and rovings hanging there in glorious color.

Curiously enough, the law came up as another thread to tie these women together. Several of the women were lawyers or studied law, are or were married to lawyers, or their boyfriends are lawyers. What does this mean? A lawyer's mind possesses an innate ability to focus, an ability that translates well into the business of color—a business that consists of

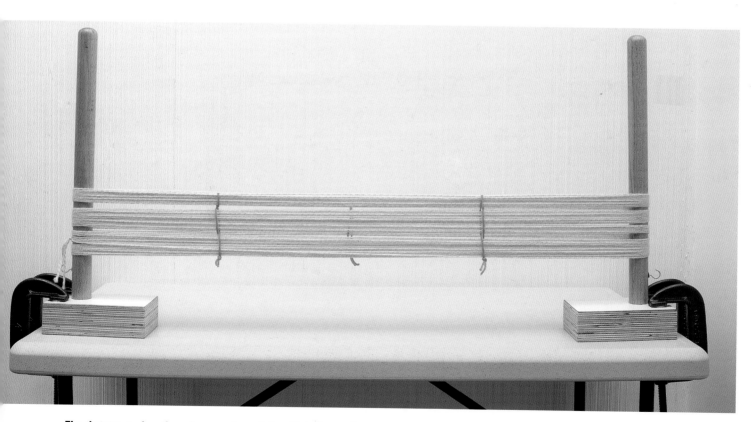

The skeining tool easily makes very long skeins. Make figure 8 ties in contrasting yarn to keep the skein tidy.

nothing *but* focus. Maie Landra (page 150) thought she had broken the thread, but then recalled that Harry, her late husband, had been a lawyer, and though she did not feel that she was a focused person, Harry kept her focused.

And this brings up another thread: They all have husbands or boyfriends who understand why they do what they do and have a great respect for their craft.

Almost all of them feel that they have arrived in a location where they will stay. If they were to move, they would build a house on the same property, or in a nearby community.

Many had not studied color theory, or textiles or painting. Others do have degrees in textiles and/or fine arts. Many of them are weavers and spinners, and they all knit.

All of them seem to have an innate sense of color. They can see color in their mind's eye and then recreate that color for their work. Some of the women talked about having color memory—the ability to see a color and later recreate the sense of that color.

All of the dyers have surrounded themselves with a peaceful environment. Running a small, hands-on business can be very stressful. Many of them have gardens, and for all of them, their environment strongly influences their color sense.

They also feel that their businesses have outgrown their space; because many of them feel it is important to try and keep work and home separate, you will not find an excess of yarn in their homes.

And they all feel that there is not enough time in the day to do everything they would like to do. They all said that they would like to be able to carve out a little bit more personal time in their day. All have said they know they will never get rich doing this, but they wouldn't trade it for anything else!

I was impressed with their level of professionalism and dedication to craft. All the dyers take great pride in their work. Dyeing is a physically difficult job, and the chemicals can be dangerous if you don't take precautions. All of the women were well aware of the toxicity of the chemicals and took great care to protect themselves from contact with the dyes and chemicals.

They listened to their bodies and were careful about repetitive motion; they were mindful about how to lift heavy pots and trays. They all plan on practicing their craft for a very long time.

I want to thank them for allowing me to interrupt their busy schedules, for their generosity, and for sharing their knowledge. I hope you will enjoy reading about these remarkable women and the glimpse you get into their lives!

The Patterns

All of the patterns in this book come from The Yarn Tree, except the patterns from Lori Lawson and Darlene Hayes. Some of the patterns were already in place when I began to write the book and have been favorites in my shop! I also designed or codesigned several new patterns. It was great fun for me to get to collaborate with some very talented people.

I applaud everyone's patience while they were learning about the design process. The number of times I asked them to redo swatches, try another stitch, or sew it "this way" could not have been easy for them. But they did it, and I think the results are really unbelievable!

I asked Lori and Darlene each to create a pattern for the book as a special project to show off what they do best. Lori loves to spin, so she dyed the roving, spun it, and then designed and knitted the Lace Gauntlets on page 48. Darlene is a natural dyer. I asked if we could do a dye project for the book with eucalyptus. She found a variety that was easily available from local florists. So while I was there, we dyed the yarn for the Ruffled Baby Socks. Both the dye recipe and pattern are available starting on page 34.

Many of the patterns are very simple, and there is a reason behind that: I strongly believe that the yarn should be allowed to speak—with a simple pattern the yarns you worked so hard to dye will be shown off to their best advantage!

On the grounds of Schaefer Yarn (page 115) there are many gardens, just one source of inspiration for her colorful yarns.

Inside the barn at Schaefer Yarn (page 115), yarn awaits the dyepot.

The Yarns

When I researched the yarns for this book, I was looking for particular qualities. Sometimes, I already had a garment in mind. Other times I let the yarn inspire me.

All of the yarns are from natural fibers—alpaca, wool, cotton, and silk. They are available through yarn stores and the Internet. Many of the manufacturers have websites that list the stores that carry their yarns (see page 154). As a yarn shop owner, I believe that there is no substitution for the knowledgeable staff at your local yarn store. So please try them first; they may even be able to order the yarn for you.

But not every store is going to carry every yarn, so we must address the question of yarn substitution. For the dyed yarns, I cannot say to you that if you substitute X for Y your yarn will dye the same as in the book. So what I recommend is that you feel free to substitute, but be sure to test, test, and test again.

For several of the knitted patterns, I searched out alternative yarns and knitted swatches to be sure that they would knit up at the same gauge, resulting in worry-free substitution for you.

There are two bits of information on the yarn label that are very important: Yards/meter per ounce/gram, and the gauge

Using a ball winder and swift, Natalie Kaire makes a skein of yarn into a ball.

(number of stitches and rows per inch). You must match this information when substituting yarns for a knit or crochet pattern. What does this mean? You need to match the thickness of the original yarn. An easy way to do that is to compare yards and ounces. If the pattern calls for a yarn that is 1¾ oz/50 g and 130 yds/119 m, then you must substitute a yarn that matches those numbers.

You must, must, must knit a test swatch to check your gauge. Your swatch *must* match the gauge of the pattern in order for the garment to come out to size. To do this you may need to change the needle size. Something I tell my students is that it was only the designer who managed to achieve that particular gauge on that particular size of needle. Everyone sitting around the table could knit with the same yarn on the same size needle and they could all have a different gauge (and they often do!).

TO MAKE A GAUGE SWATCH

Cast on 20 stitches, and knit for 4" (10cm) in the pattern stitch.

Measure across the middle of the swatch (you do not want to measure near the cast-on edge or right under the needles) and count the number of stitches. Divide the number of stitches by the width.

Measure just below the needles to just above the cast-on edge and count the number of rows. Divide the number of rows by the height in inches.

Voila, you have your gauge.

For example, if 20 stitches and 36 rows = 4" (10cm), you have 5 stitches and 9 rows to the inch.

How to Prepare the Work Area

I am fortunate enough to have a separate studio for my dyeing. I realize that is not the case for everyone, and that many of you may be dyeing in your kitchen. Every dyer I interviewed for this book began in the kitchen, so don't despair!

Here is how I prepare my work area: Let's start with the work table. Lay down plastic sheeting or large trash bags, and on top of that place newspaper or Kraft paper. The newspaper helps to absorb any spills, and the plastic sheeting helps to keep your table clean from stains. (Keep paper towels handy for mopping up excess dye and any spills that might occur.) Place plastic wrap on top of the newspaper or Kraft paper, overlapping them in the center of the table.

The area where you will mix your dye must be free of any open windows or fans. The dye powder is very fine and can be carried a long way by the slightest movement in the air. You should not measure out your dye in the vicinity of any foodstuff or eating/cooking utensils. Some people will put down slightly damp newspaper or paper towels where they will measure out the dye powder to catch any stray particles, then immediately roll up this paper and toss it out—an excellent idea!

When you are cleaning up, be sure that your sink is free of any household dishes or pots and pans. I found that Clorox Clean-Up is a big help in removing any stains from the dyes that splash onto your sink. To get the dye off your skin, use Reduran.

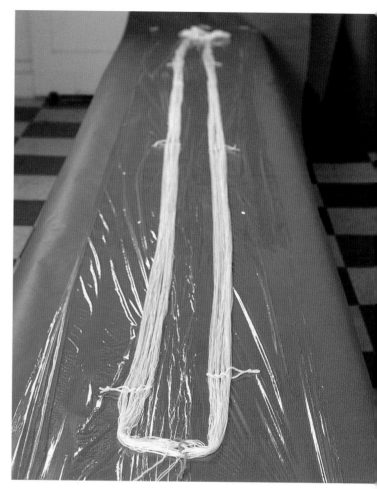

Keeping your work surface clean is of utmost importance. A layer of Kraft paper under plastic wrap helps protect the work surface.

unsweetened kool-aid and food coloring

This chapter covers two easy dye projects that you and your children can do together. One uses unsweetened Kool-Aid, the other food coloring. Both give rich beautiful colors! The only other ingredient you need is distilled white vinegar.

At The Yarn Tree we teach two different Kool-Aid/Food Coloring Workshops in conjunction with classes. The spinners dye roving and the weavers dye yarn. For the participants it is a time to play with color, and everyone really seems to enjoy it!

unsweetened kool-aid–dyed wool

MATERIALS

- 1 Skein Periwinkle Yarn from Henry's Attic, 100% wool, 8 oz (226g), 250 yds (228m)
- Synthrapol
- Distilled white vinegar
- Unsweetened Kool-Aid in the following flavors: Tropical Punch, 6 packages; Cherry, 2 packages

TOOLS

- Measuring spoons
- Measuring cup
- Enamel or stainless steel pot
- Mixing spoon
- Candy thermometer
- Nitrile gloves
- Reduran
- Apron and pot holders
- Paper towels
- Basin

I thought it would be fun to go down the block to my friend Maggie's house and do a little Kool-Aid dyeing with her kids, Toni and Slade. Toni learned to knit last year and has become quite an accomplished knitter.

Kool-Aid dyeing is fun, safe, and easy to do. You can use your everyday household utensils and pots when dyeing with Kool-Aid. Kool-Aid can be purchased at your local grocery store in a variety of flavors (colors).

It is important to supervise your children while they are at the stove and working with pots of hot water. Speaking of pots of hot water, you *never* want to let the water boil—this will ruin your wool. Kool-Aid will dye only protein fibers—wool, silk, alpaca, mohair, etc. It will not dye cellulosic fibers—cotton, rayon, linen, hemp, etc.

prepare the yarn

1. In a dishpan, soak the yarn in 4 qt (4L) warm water with ½ tsp (2.5mL) Synthrapol and ½ cup (120mL) vinegar for 1 hour.

prepare the dyepot

2. Place 8 qt (8L) water and 1 cup (250mL) vinegar in the dyepot.

3. Add the packets of unsweetened Kool-Aid, stir well, and increase the heat to bring the water up to 185°F (85°C).

add the yarn

4. Add the presoaked yarn and carefully stir to ensure that all the yarn gets into the Kool-Aid dyebath.

5. Bring the water back up to 185°F (85°C), and maintain this temperature until the water goes clear. This should only take 10–15 minutes. If the dyebath

STEP 2

STEP 3

STEP 4

STEP 5

STEP 6

STEP 6 (CONTINUED)

has not gone clear, you can add ¼ cup (60mL) vinegar (hold the yarn out of the way to ensure that the vinegar doesn't get directly on it). Maintain the temperature, and if after another 10 minutes the water has not gone clear, turn the heat off. You may have more dyestuff in the pot than the yarn can absorb.

remove the yarn

6. Remove the yarn from the pot or allow the pot to cool to room temperature.

7. Rinse the yarn in warm water and ¼ tsp (1.25mL) Synthrapol. Then rinse the yarn two or three times in clear water. Allow to air dry.

8. Once the skein is dry, stretch it back out under tension and wind it into a ball.

Tip Use Reduran to remove the Kool-Aid from your hands.

thick 'n' thin scarf

SKILL LEVEL
Beginner

MATERIALS
- 1 Skein Periwinkle from Henry's Attic, 100% wool, 8 oz (226g), 250 yds (226m)
- 1 pair US #11 (8mm) straight needles

GAUGE
- In garter stitch
- 12 stitches = 4" (10cm)

SIZE
Approximately 6" (15cm) wide by 80" (203cm) long

DESIGNED BY LINDA LA BELLE

instructions

Cast on 18 stitches and knit until you have 36" (91cm) of yarn left.

Bind off loosely. It is best to use a larger needle to bind off if you have one!

Weave in the ends.

food coloring–dyed wool/mohair

MATERIALS

- **2 skeins Green Mountain Spinnery Mountain Mohair, 70% wool, 30% mohair, 2 oz (56 g), 140 yds (128m) each, color Edelweiss**
- **1 skein left as is, the other wound into a skein 10 yds (9m) in diameter.**
- **Synthrapol**
- **Distilled white vinegar**
- **McCormick Food Colors in the following colors: Blue, Neon Blue**

TOOLS

- **Measuring spoons**
- **Measuring cups**
- **Scissors**
- **Mixing spoon**
- **Enamel or stainless steel pot**
- **Plastic wrap**
- **Acrylic yarn**

As a collector of textiles, I am fascinated with the ikat technique. This is a method used to dye the yarns prior to weaving fabric by tying off areas of the warp and/or weft yarns to resist taking up the dye. This technique is practiced by many cultures. In Indonesia it is used to tell a story, in Central Asia silk coats blaze with color, and in Japan it is done on silk yarn that is finer than most human hair. Saris in India, rebozos from Central Mexico, and woven fabrics from South America and Southeast Asia all use an ikat technique.

Here is my humble homage to this centuries-old technique using plastic wrap and food coloring. Food coloring is simple to use, but a word of warning: The colors are very concentrated, so a little bit goes a long way. Just as with Kool-Aid dyeing, you can use your everyday utensils and pots.

I chose this wool/mohair blend from the Green Mountain Spinnery because I love the way the combination of fibers takes up the dye. The mohair will "halo" (come to the surface) and seem to glow. As you will see on page 31, there are three different sets of mittens. I dyed three different colors of the same yarn with the same color formula. I wanted you to see how differently the color formula dyed these yarns. I used Edelweiss (a natural white), Pistachio (previously dyed by the manufacturer), and Blizzard (a natural gray).

prepare the yarn

1. In a dishpan, soak both skeins in a solution of 4 qt (4L) warm water (120°F [49°C]) with ½ tsp (2.5mL) Synthrapol and ½ cup (120mL) vinegar for 1 hour.

2. Tear a strip of plastic wrap approximately 3" (7.5cm) wide. Cut this strip into pieces ranging from 1–3" (2.5–7.5cm) wide. Repeat until you have 40 small pieces of plastic wrap.

3. Cut 80 strands of acrylic yarn 6" (15cm) long.

4. Remove the long skein and gently squeeze out any excess water. Stretch the skein out around whatever you made it on.

5. Take a piece of the plastic wrap that you have prepared and wrap the skein as shown. Take two of the acrylic ties you have prepared and tie one at each end of the plastic wrap. Pull tight but *do not* tie a square knot (instead of tying the acrylic tie twice, tie it only once). Repeat this process in random order around the skein, varying the distance between the wrappings. The less planned, the more the yarn will knit up like clouds!

6. If the skein feels dry, return it to the soak solution while you prepare the dyepot.

prepare the dyepot

7. In the dyepot place 6 qt (6L) water, 1/2 cup (120mL) vinegar, 10 drops Blue food coloring, and 20 drops Neon Blue food coloring. Stir well.

add the yarn

8. Bring the pot up to 190°F (88°C). Drop both skeins of yarn in the pot and stir gently. Bring back up to temperature and maintain this temperature until the water goes clear. *Do not* allow the pot to boil! If the dyebath has not gone clear after 15 minutes, you can add 1/4 cup (60mL) distilled white vinegar (hold the yarn out of the way to ensure that the vinegar doesn't get on it). Maintain the temperature, and if after another 10 minutes the water has not gone clear, turn the heat off. You may have more dyestuff in the pot than the yarn can absorb. Allow the yarn to cool completely in the pot.

remove the yarn

9. Remove both skeins. The shorter one can be rinsed at this point; the longer one needs to have the wrapping removed.

10. Stretch the long skein back out. Snip one tail of the acrylic close to the plastic wrap, then pull on the other tail and it will come right off. Repeat for the other tie, and unwrap the plastic wrap. Continue to do this until all the plastic wrap has been removed.

11. Rinse the skein in warm water and 1/4 tsp (1.25mL) Synthrapol. Then rinse two or three times more. Allow to air dry.

12. Once the skeins are dry, stretch them back out under tension and wind into balls.

STEP 5

STEP 8

STEP 10

cloud mittens

DESIGNED BY LINDA LA BELLE

Mittens are one of my favorite things to knit. They knit up quickly and make a great gift! The organic, cloudlike shapes from this dye process knit up into a pair of mittens that are unique. If you want to make the mittens a little bigger, go up a needle size, a little smaller, go down a needle size.

striped color pattern

Work 2 rounds using solid color yarn, Main Color (MC).

Work 3 rounds using two-color yarn, Contrast Color (CC).

Note Be sure to twist your yarns when changing colors by picking up the new color from beneath the previous color. This prevents holes from forming.

instructions (make 2)

Using the US #6 (4mm) needles and MC, cast on 44 stitches. Transfer the stitches to the US #4 (3.5mm) double-pointed needles, and distribute evenly over three of the needles (14, 16, 14). Join, being careful not to twist the stitches.

Note Your cast-on row counts as Rnd 1.

Observing the color pattern above, work as follows:

Work 28 rounds in k1, p1 ribbing.

Decrease Rnd (Rnd 30) *K9, k2tog*; repeat from * to * three more times (40 sts).

Switch to the US #5 (3.75mm) double-pointed needles, and begin the Thumb Gusset.

thumb gusset

Rnd 31 K1, place first marker, M1L, k1, M1R. Place second marker. Knit to end of round.

Rnd 32 Knit.

Rnd 33 Knit.

Work these 3 rounds 5 times more for a total of 18 rounds, always increasing after first marker and before second marker until there are 13 sts between markers.

Rnd 49 or Next Rnd K1, place 13 sts on holder, inc 1 stitch. Knit to end of round (40 sts). (Pull yarn tight after that first stitch and before and after you increase to avoid a gap.)

Knit 25 rounds (or until mitten reaches the top of your pinky).

top of mitten

Rnd 74 or Next Rnd *K4, k2og*; repeat from * to * to end of round, ending k4.

Knit 4 rounds.

SKILL LEVEL
Intermediate

MATERIALS
- 2 skeins Green Mountain Spinnery Mountain Mohair, 70% wool, 30% mohair, 2 oz (56g), 140 yds (128m) each, one dyed solid (MC), the other dyed via the faux ikat technique (CC)
- 1 set US #4 (3.5mm) double-pointed needles (for the ribbing)
- 1 set US #5 (3.75mm) double-pointed needles (for the hand of the mitten)
- 1 pair US #6 (4mm) straight needles (for casting on)
- tapestry needle
- stitch markers
- stitch holder

GAUGE
- In stockinette stitch on US #5 needles
- 24 stitches and 36 rows = 4" (10cm)

SIZE
To fit an average adult hand

Abbreviations & Techniques

k2tog Knit 2 stitches together.

knit pick up With the right side (outside) of the work facing you, insert the right-hand needle under the two strands of the edge stitch, wrap your yarn

(continued on far right column)

Rnd 79 or Next Rnd *K3, k2tog*; repeat from * to * to end of round, ending k4.

Knit 3 rounds.

Rnd 83 or Next Rnd *K2, k2tog*; repeat from * to * to end of round, ending k4.

Knit 2 rounds.

Rnd 86 or Next Rnd *K1, k2tog*; repeat from * to * to end of round, ending k4.

Knit 1 round.

Rnd 88 or Next Rnd K2tog to the end of the round.

Cut a long tail, thread a tapestry needle, and run through remaining stitches.

(Hint: If you run the needle in the same direction as you would be knitting, the hole will close up very nicely. I recommend running it through twice). Bring the tail to the wrong side and weave it in on a diagonal.

thumb

Place the 13 sts from the holder onto three needles, join yarn, and knit pick up 5 sts in the gap between the first and the last stitch (18 sts).

Knit 18 rounds (or until mitten thumb length is to the middle of your thumbnail).

Next Rnd *K1, k2tog*; repeat from * to * to end of round.

Knit 1 round.

Next Rnd *K2tog*; repeat from * to * to end of round.

finishing

Cut a long tail, and pull through stitches as above.

Weave in the ends.

(continued from left column)

and knit. This will put a new stitch on your right-hand needle. Continue in this manner, working from right to left, until you have the desired number of stitches.

M1L With the tip of left needle, lift strand between last stitch knitted and next stitch on left-hand needle, from front to back. Knit into the back of it to increase 1 stitch.

M1R With tip of left needle, lift strand between last stitch knitted and next stitch on left-hand needle, from back to front. Knit into the front of it to increase 1 stitch.

SIMPLE YARN SUBSTITUTION

If you like the pattern for the mittens, but you do not wish to dye the yarn, you can substitute any two colors from The Green Mountain Spinnery Mountain Mohair line of yarn.

DARLENE HAYES, HAND JIVE KNITS

Some time ago my friend Takako Ueki of HABU Textiles told me about Darlene Hayes. I was immediately taken with the fact that Darlene is a gatherer of natural dyestuff. This was someone I definitely wanted to know!

When I arrived in Davis, California, a heatwave had just broken, and the weather was perfect. Darlene has the luxury of being able to dye outdoors; she has set up her dyepots in the side yard, a few feet from her garden, and that day Darlene was dyeing with cochineal. This is a red dye that comes from an insect native to Mexico and South America, living on the Opuntia cactus. Although the insect is farmed today, it is still gathered by hand. Cochineal is a strong dye, and Darlene is able to use the dyestock at least three times. She will get a dark red with the first batch of yarn, and it will get subsequently lighter with each batch, until a pale pink is produced.

The next day, Darlene prepared to dye with eucalyptus she had gathered and allowed to dry for several months. The dried leaves are placed in a porous bag and simmered, covered, for two hours, then left overnight. The next morning, Darlene will bring the pot to a boil and allow it to simmer covered for another two hours. Eucalyptus is a substantive dye (no additives are required for permanent color), so the scoured (prewashed) skeins could go right into the dyepot. The color takes immediately.

Darlene periodically stirs the pot and checks the color. Once the color is to Darlene's liking, she will remove that batch of yarn from the pot and introduce another batch of scoured yarn to the pot. This second batch will come out more of a buttery yellow.

When I saw her, Darlene had recently switched her business from retail to exclusively wholesale. She realized that to meet the demand for her yarn, she would have to dye 30 pounds (13.6kg) of yarn a day! No easy task by oneself. At some point Darlene would like to hire help, but right now she is doing it alone.

She is the ultimate multitasker. While yarn is in the dyepot, another 30 pounds (13.6kg) is being mordanted, more is being rinsed, skeins are hanging to dry, and dyestock is cooking. But it doesn't stop there—in the afternoon,

when it is too hot to work outside, she is in the house getting the skeins of yarn ready to be mordanted or she is twisting and labeling skeins of dried yarn.

The day's work done, we went for a walk along the bike path near Darlene's home. Here she pointed out the black walnuts, oak galls, and olives that she will gather in the fall. She told me her friends allow her to gather eucalyptus, mullein, and Queen Anne's Lace from their property. She will also go up to the eastern side of the Sierra Nevadas to backpack and harvest sage brush and rabbit brush.

Darlene learned to knit as a teenager. While studying botany in college, Darlene took a class in costume design. It was then that Darlene began to work with natural dyes. She went on to a career as a research scientist and then a patent attorney. Ready for a third career, she fell back on the two things that had kept her interest over the years: knitting and natural dyeing.

Darlene started Hand Jive with the idea of being a knitwear designer and selling patterns through her website and to yarn stores. Having a difficult time finding yarns she liked, she

thought, "Why don't I just dye my own?" After signing up for a workshop with Luisa Gelenter of La Lana Wools in the fall of 2001 in Taos, New Mexico, she spent the summer before the class experimenting with everything she could lay her hands on, keeping meticulous notes on all her experimentation. On her return from Taos, Darlene began to sell her hand-dyed yarns both wholesale and retail through her website and at trade shows.

Darlene started out dyeing her signature fingering-weight yarn, but has begun to branch out: The newest are a thick-and-thin yarn and an organic wool from Montana-raised Columbia sheep.

I asked Darlene what it is about dyeing with plants that attracts her, and she told me she likes the plants, the mystery of the plants, and the fact that it is not measuring out by teaspoons and tablespoons—the organic nature of the process.

In the future, Darlene and her partner, Eric, plan on moving to family property in the wine country of northern California. There they will build a home and a dye studio, and plant a dyer's garden. Darlene's goal is to find more time to design with the yarns she dyes.

THIS PAGE, CLOCKWISE FROM TOP LEFT: One rose of many flowers in Darlene's garden. Darlene stirs 5 pounds (2.26kg) of eucalyptus-dyed yarn. Dried eucalyptus gathered by Darlene is ready to go into the dyepot. Darlene Hayes at the gate to her work area. OPPOSITE PAGE, LEFT TO RIGHT: As you can see, Darlene's environment has a strong influence on her color sense; here she hangs yarn to dry that has been dyed with cochineal. Darlene's signature yarn, Nature's Palette Fingering Weight Yarn, is lushly dyed with a variety of natural dyes.

"I love the organic nature of the process."

fresh eucalyptus–dyed wool

MATERIALS

- **Fingering weight 100% wool yarn, 1³/₄ oz (50g), 175 yds (160m)**
- **Synthrapol**
- **Potassium aluminum sulfate (alum) (pickling alum from the grocery store is fine)**
- **E. Pulverulenta (eucalyptus)—be sure that the eucalyptus is fresh (dried eucalyptus has been treated with glycerin) and that it has no dyes or wax on it**

TOOLS

- **Enamel or stainless steel pot**
- **Candy thermometer**
- **Mixing spoon**
- **Measuring spoons**
- **Measuring cups**
- **Pot holders**
- **Dust mask**
- **Gloves**

I had come to Darlene's studio with a specific request—that we do a project for the book with a plant that could be obtained anywhere, any time of the year. My thought had been eucalyptus. If you don't have it in your backyard, your florist can get it for you, or you can purchase it online.

Darlene was good enough to search out an easily obtainable species, *E. Pulverulenta* to be exact. Our experiment got off to a bit of a bumpy start—the florist had ordered in the wrong species! But Darlene made a few calls, and we found a wholesale florist nearby who had just what we were looking for. So we hopped in the car and picked up our eucalyptus, and got right to dyeing with it!

Earlier I said eucalyptus does not need a mordant, but the following recipe calls for a mordant (alum). Why? *The E. Pulverulenta* we used was a new variety for Darlene, and she wasn't sure how the yarn would take the color. As we had no time for testing, we knew that by using a mordant the yarn would accept the dyestuff.

Note This project is a two-day process. On the first day you will presoak and then mordant your yarn. You will also begin the dyestock.

prepare the yarn

1. Presoak the yarn by placing the skein in warm water with two drops of Synthrapol for 1 hour. Remove and squeeze out any excess water.

2. In a small enamel or stainless steel pot (your dyepot), place 4 quarts (4L) warm water (110°F [43°C]). While wearing a dust mask and gloves, measure out 1¼ tsp (6.25g) of alum into a glass measuring cup, add ¼ cup (60mL) boiling water, and stir well to dissolve. Pour this into the dyepot. Add the presoaked yarn.

3. Slowly bring the water in the pot to 185°F (85°C) over 45 minutes. Do not let the pot boil.

4. Once you reach 185°F (85°C), hold at this temperature for 1 hour. Allow to cool to room temperature. (This may take several hours.)

5. Remove the skein, squeeze out any excess water, and place in a ziplock bag so it doesn't dry out overnight.

prepare the dyestock

6. Strip the leaves off 4 stalks of eucalyptus. You may want to wear gardening gloves or the like while doing this.

7. Rinse the pot and place 4 qt (4L) warm water (110°F [43°C]) into the pot along with the eucalyptus leaves.

8. Bring to a boil and simmer covered for 2 hours. Turn off the heat and allow to sit overnight.

9. The next day, turn the heat back on under the dyepot and bring to a boil. Simmer covered for 2 hours. You will notice that the dyestock is darker in color than it was the day before. Cool the pot to room temperature and then strain out the dyestock, throw out the leaves, rinse the pot, and pour the dyestock back into the pot.

add the yarn

10. Bring the pot back up to a boil. Turn off the heat, add the mordanted skein, and allow to sit for 1 hour.

remove the yarn

11. Remove the yarn from the pot and gently squeeze out any excess liquid. Soak the skein in cool water with 2–3 drops Synthrapol, then rinse with clear water 2–3 times. Allow the skein to dry.

12. Once dry, stretch it back out under tension and wind it into a ball.

STEP 6

STEP 7

STEP 8

STEP 9

STEP 10

STEP 11

ruffled baby socks

SKILL LEVEL
Intermediate

MATERIALS

- Approximately 67 (93, 118) yds (61 [85, 108]m) fingering-weight yarn (model shown in Nature's Palette Fingering Weight Merino in ripe wheat [NP-118])

- 1 set of 5 US #3 (3.25mm) double-pointed needles

- 1 set of 5 US #5 (3.75mm) double-pointed needles

- 1 US D-3 (3.25mm) crochet hook

- tapestry needle

- 2 stitch markers

GAUGE

- In stockinette stitch with US #3 needles

- 28 stitches = 4" (10cm)

SIZES
0-3 (3-6, 6-9) months

Abbreviations & Techniques

k2tog Knit 2 stitches together.

p2tog Purl 2 stitches together.

sk2tog Slip 1 stitch knitwise, put it back on the left needle, knit 2 stitches together.

yo (yarn over) This is simply the act of bringing the yarn forward as if to purl, then following your pattern directions. For this pattern, after your yarn over, it calls for you to k1. So bring your yarn

(continued on far right column)

DESIGNED BY DARLENE HAYES OF HAND JIVE

Darlene had asked me what kind of pattern I would like from her for the book. Upon seeing the beautiful buttery yellow the eucalyptus can produce, and knowing Darlene's penchant for designing socks, I asked her to design a baby bootie. She came up with this easy-to-knit sock; I love the crochet ruffle on the edge!

instructions (make 2)

Note This sock is worked from the top down.

Using the US #3 needles, cast on 28 (32, 36) stitches. Join into a round, being careful not to twist the stitches.

Work in k1, p1 ribbing until the ribbing measures 2 (2½, 3)" (5 [6.5, 7.5]cm).

heel flap

Slip the next st purlwise, then k13. Put the remaining stitches in the round on a piece of waste yarn or a stitch holder, to be used later for the instep, and continue with the 14 sts just worked. Turn the piece. Slip the first st purlwise, p13. Continue working the heel flap in stockinette stitch, slipping the first stitch in each row, until the flap measures 1 (1¼, 1½)" (2.5 [3, 3.8]cm).

heel turn

Slip 1 st, k8 (9, 10) sts, sk2tog, k1, turn; slip 1 st, p5, p2tog, p1, turn; *slip 1 st, knit to 1 st before the gap, sk2tog, k1, turn; slip 1 st, purl to 1 st before the gap, p2tog, p1. Repeat from * until all the sts have been used.

gusset

Slip 1 st. Knit heel sts. Knit pick up 6 (7, 8) sts along one edge of the heel flap. Knit the first reserved instep stitch, and place a stitch marker. Knit to the last instep st, and place a stitch marker. K1, pick up 6 (7, 8) sts along the other edge of the heel flap.

Rnd 1 Knit to 2 sts before the first stitch marker, k2tog. Knit to second stitch marker, sk2tog. Knit to end of round.

Rnd 2 Knit.

Work these two rounds until you have reduced the number of stitches to 28 (32, 36).

foot

Continue working in stockinette stitch until the sock measures 2½ (3, 3½)" (6.5 [7.5, 9]cm) from the back of the heel. You may need to adjust this length a bit depending on the baby you are making these for, so use your best judgment.

star toe

Rnd 1 Divide the stitches evenly onto four double-pointed needles. *Knit to 2 sts before the end of the needle, k2tog; repeat from * for the remaining three needles.

Rnd 2 Knit.

Work these two rounds until you have 14 (16, 18) sts remaining.

Work Rnd 1 until you have 6 (8, 6) sts remaining.

Cut the yarn, thread it onto a tapestry needle, and then draw it through the remaining stitches. Pull the yarn tight, and then secure the end on the inside of the sock.

ruffled edge

The socks are worn with the cuff turned down, so the cuff is worked on the wrong side of the sock. Turn the sock inside out. Pick up but do not work (see note at right) 28 (32, 36) sts around the top of the ribbing, distributing the stitches on 4 needles.

Using the US #5 needles, work one round of k1, yo all the way around. You will have doubled the number of stitches (56 [64, 72] sts).

Purl 1 round.

For the bind-off, take the crochet hook and insert it into the first stitch in the round. Draw a loop of yarn through, dropping the stitch from the knitting needle, and then chain 3 stitches. *Insert the hook into the next stitch on the needle, dropping it from the needle. Draw a loop of yarn through this stitch, and then through the last stitch in the chain; chain 3 stitches. Repeat from * until all of the stitches have been bound off. Fasten off the last stitch. Darn in all loose ends.

(continued from left column)

forward as if to purl, now you will knit the first stitch on your left needle.

You will notice that the working yarn comes back over the top of your needle from the front of your work. This is correct. It will create another stitch on your needle (an increase) and what looks like a hole in your work (the lacy open stitch).

pick up but do not work Place the tip of the needle through a purl bump, placing that loop on the needle. (It is easier if you use a very small needle.) Continue until you have the required number of stitches on the needles. Join the yarn.

3

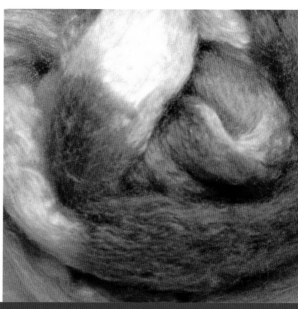

ashford wool dyes

The idea for searching out a cold dye method came from Rachel DeNys. She knitted a pair of white lace gloves for her wedding in fingering-weight organic wool, and wanting to continue to wear them, she thought to dye the gloves. The problem she faced was that the gloves fit snugly on her hands. Most dye methods require heat, which can cause shrinkage. I didn't know about the cold pad method at that time, so we dyed the gloves in an indigo bath. When I started to do research for this book, I thought about Rachel's dilemma and decided to try to find a cold dye method.

After testing recipes where I made my own cold pad dyestuff, I found the Ashford Wool Dyes and their Cold Pad Mix. I was very impressed with its ease of use. I found that we had minimal shrinkage with this method of dyeing!

Both items in this chapter were knitted first and then dyed in the cold pad method. We used two very different substrates, a worsted weight mohair/wool blend and very fine laceweight cashmere.

ashford cold pad–dyed mohair/wool hat

MATERIALS

- Feather Lace Hat knit from pattern on page 42.
- 5¼ oz (150g) urea
- Rubbing alcohol
- 1½ tsp (7.5mL) Polycell
- Dishwashing liquid (I used Dawn)
- Distilled white vinegar
- Ashford Wool Dye, color Rust

TOOLS

- Dust mask
- Gloves
- Measuring spoons
- Measuring cups
- Small whisks
- 3 wide-mouth jars with lids, 2-cup size (500mL)
- 3" (7.5cm) sponge brush
- Plastic wrap or large ziplock bag
- Bowl for soaking hat

STEP 7

STEP 8

STEP 9

I originally had no intention of including the Feather Lace Hat in the book. When the Ashford Wool Dyes arrived, and I needed an already knit item to test the dye on, Tara Swanson knit up the hat for me in what seemed a flash. I was so impressed with how this yarn took the dye that I decided to include it!

Note The padding mix should be made up 24 hours ahead of time. Sometimes the mix comes out lumpy, but if you let it sit overnight the lumps will disappear.

prepare the padding mixture

1. In a jar place 5¼ oz (150g) urea. Pour in 1 cup (250mL) boiling water and stir until dissolved, then add 1 cup (250mL) cold water.

2. Add 1 tsp (5mL) rubbing alcohol, and sprinkle 1½ tsp (7.5mL) Polycell into the mixture, stirring vigorously. Add 2 drops dishwashing liquid and 1 tbsp (15mL) vinegar, and stir well. After the padding mixture has cooled,

seal the jar and allow to sit overnight, keeping it sealed until needed.

prepare the piece

3. In a separate bowl, soak the hat for 1 hour in warm water with 2 drops dishwashing liquid. While the hat is soaking, mix up your dyestock.

prepare the dye paste

4. Wearing your dust mask and gloves, place ½ tsp (2.5g) dye powder in a jar, add a little cold water, and mix well to make a paste. Add 2 cups (500mL) warm water and stir until the granules dissolve. Set aside for at least 30 minutes to rest.

prepare the dyestock

5. Pour 1¼ cup (300mL) padding mixture into the third jar, add 6 tbsp (90mL) dyestock, and stir well.

6. Remove your hat from the soak solution and gently squeeze out the excess

water. Place the hat on plastic wrap on your work surface.

paint the piece

7. Using the 3" (7.5cm) sponge brush, paint the entire surface of the hat, pressing on the hat with the brush, being sure to give good coverage.

8. Turn the hat over and paint the other side. Turn the hat inside out and repeat.

9. Once you are satisfied with the coverage, seal the hat in plastic wrap or a large ziplock bag and set in a warm spot to cure. This can be a sunny windowsill or near a radiator. I left the sample hat to cure for 48 hours.

10. Soak the hat in cold water for 10 minutes, then very gently (*no* agitation) wash the hat in warm water and dishwashing liquid 2–3 times. Rinse in warm water, gently squeeze out excess water, and dry flat in the shade. If you wish, you can block this hat out a bit so that the lace will open up.

feather lace hat

DESIGNED BY KIMBERLY KAUFFMAN

SKILL LEVEL
Intermediate to Advanced

MATERIALS
- 1 skein Sweet Grass Wool Montana Mohair, 70% Wool, 30% Mohair, 4 oz (113g), 230 yds (210m)
- 1 16" (40.5cm) US #8 (5mm) circular needle
- 1 set US #8 (5mm) double-pointed needles
- stitch marker
- tapestry needle

GAUGE
- In stockinette stitch
- 19 stitches = 4" (10cm)

SIZE
To fit a 20" (50cm) head

Abbreviations & Techniques

k2tog Knit 2 stitches together.

ssk (slip, slip, knit) This is a directional decrease. Individually slip the first two stitches from the left needle to the right, going into each stitch as if to knit (putting a twist in the stitch). Making sure that your working yarn is to the back of your work, take your left needle and insert the tip of that needle into the front of the two stitches that you just slipped to the right hand needle. Now knit those two stitches together.

yo (yarn over) This is simply the act of bringing the yarn forward as if to purl,

(continued on page 44)

Kim designed this hat several years ago for my shop. We had just gotten in the Sweet Grass yarn and wanted to see how it would knit up. Kim did such a great job designing it that the Beginning Knitters, with a little help, are able to make it for their second project. Kim has since moved to the Philadelphia area and is busy raising a family. She is missed at The Yarn Tree.

instructions

Using the circular needle, cast on 91 stitches.

With yarn in the back and being careful not to twist the stitches, slip the last cast-on stitch onto the left-hand needle, so it sits next to the first stitch (the slip knot). Place a marker to mark the beginning of the round on the right-hand needle. Knit the first 2 stitches on the left hand needle together. Pull the yarn firmly to prevent a gap. (On each round, when you come to the marker, just slip it to the right needle and keep working.) (90 sts)

Rnd 1 Knit.

Rnd 2 Purl.

Rnd 3 Knit.

Rnd 4 Purl.

Rnd 5 Knit.

Rnd 6 Purl.

Rnd 7 Knit.

Rnd 8 Knit.

Rnd 9 K1 *yo, k2, ssk, k2tog, k2, yo, k1*; repeat from * to * 8 more times. You will have 8 sts left; end yo, k2, ssk, k2tog, k2, yo.

Note Be aware of where your final yarn over is on Rnd 9. When you go from Rnd 9 to Rnd 10, make sure that the last yarn over of Rnd 9 remains behind the marker. If not, it will throw the pattern off.

Rnd 10 Knit.

Rnd 11 *Yo, k2, ssk, k2tog, k2, yo, k1*; repeat from * to * 9 more times.

Rnd 12 Knit.

Repeat Rnds 9 through 12 until work measures 6.5" (16.5cm) from cast-on edge, ending with Rnd 12.

(continued from page 43)

then following your pattern. For this pattern, after your yarn over it calls for you to knit. So bring your yarn forward as if to purl. Now knit the next stitch. You will notice that the working yarn comes back over the top of your needle from the front of your work. This is correct. It will create another stitch on your needle (an increase) and what looks like a hole in your work (the lacy open stitch).

SIMPLE YARN SUBSTITUTION

If you fell in love with the Feather Lace Hat, but do not wish to dye the yarn, I found the perfect substitution yarn. It is New England Highland from Harrisville Designs, Inc., 100% wool, 3¹/₂ oz (100g), 200 yds (183m). We were able to keep the same needle size and match the gauge. The sample swatch for the Highland yarn is knit up in "Rose."

decrease

Rnd 1 *K7, k2tog*; repeat from * to * to end of round (80 sts).

Rnd 2 Knit.

Rnd 3 *K6, k2tog*; repeat from * to * to end of round (70 sts).

Rnd 4 Knit.

Rnd 5 *K5, k2tog*; repeat from * to * to end of round (60 sts).

Rnd 6 Knit.

Switch to double-pointed needles.

Rnd 7 *K4, k2tog*; repeat from * to * to end of round (50 sts).

Rnd 8 *K3, k2tog*; repeat from * to * to end of round (40 sts).

Rnd 9 *K2, k2tog*; repeat from * to * to end of round (30 sts).

Rnd 10 *K1, k2tog*; repeat from * to * to end of round (20 sts).

Rnd 11 K2tog; repeat to end of round (10 sts).

finishing

Cut a long tail, draw it through the remaining stitches twice, and pull tight to close the top of the hat. Weave in all the ends.

LORI LAWSON, CAPISTRANO FIBER ARTS

Lori Lawson has the smallest operation of all the dyers I interviewed. She works from her home in San Juan Capistrano, California, selling her handpainted yarns and rovings to only two stores (one being The Yarn Tree!), and does several high-end arts-and-crafts shows in the Orange County area.

Lori learned to spin before she began dyeing, and before she learned to spin, she learned to weave. She began dyeing after she and a friend had bought some roving over the Internet. After spinning it up, they weren't very happy. Looking at the newly spun yarn, Lori and her friend, Margie, realized they could do it better! Lori ordered acid dyes and some Merino roving, dyed it themselves, and they were more than happy with the results. She bought more fibers, dyed and spun them, and was hooked!

Lori has been dyeing for six years now and has added handspun, hand-dyed yarns along with handknit items made from those yarns to her repertoire. Felters have begun to take notice of her beautiful rovings as well. In the fall, Lori goes to two craft shows, where she sells her handknits, handwovens, and handpainted yarns and fibers.

Lori started out as a lawyer—I feel that the focus she had as a lawyer translates well to her business as dyer. I asked her if she would like to expand her business, but she's not ready to do that yet—she doesn't want employees in her home, and she doesn't yet want to move her operation to a studio away from her home.

She just loves what she is doing, and her face lights up when she talks about her work. Lori told me that when she is dyeing the roving, she is already anticipating how it will look when spun up. She actually gets impatient, but she knows she has to wait for all the steps of the process to be completed.

Her studio, the sunroom off her house, overlooks the pool and gardens, blue skies, and palm trees. (The best part is that when it gets too hot, she can jump in her pool to cool off!) As we hung the rovings out to dry on wooden drying racks I could immediately see the

CLOCKWISE FROM TOP: Lori Lawson spins fiber she handpainted. Once the sunroom, Lori's studio gets amazing light! Lori knits.

influence the environment had on her. The colors in nature are her strongest inspiration. The very first colorway she designed was named Laguna Canyon: It was springtime, and the canyon was a riot of colors. Often when she is painting one colorway she begins to see another—she jots down notes, and as

"You must allow enough time for the colors to take."

soon as she can, she works on the new one. She uses only natural fibers—silk, angora, merino wool, cashmere, and blends, to name a few. Today she uses more commercially spun yarns, because she just can't keep up with the spinning.

Lori's secret about dyeing: "Time is the most important thing. Whether it be steaming or immersion, you must allow enough time for the colors to take." Her advice is to start out small—don't make a big investment. Do something as simple as Kool-Aid or food coloring dyeing first.

Lori and I talked as she painted the roving. I was very impressed with what a tidy dyer she is. She feels it's important to be neat for safety reasons. She is a meticulous note-taker (I'm sure from her years in law!): She started out with notebooks, but has reduced the note-taking to index cards. The notes are dated and have all the color info and a sample of the painted roving. This way she can easily re-create a colorway.

Although Lori and her husband Paul do not have pets, they take great care of the insects in their garden. While I was there, two monarch butterfly chrysalises were about to open, and a horned tomato worm was living in the grape arbor. Morning and evening, we would all go out to check on these fascinating insects.

The icing on the cake was getting to watch Lori spin up and then knit with roving she had dyed. It was a lovely ending to a great day!

lace gauntlets

SKILL LEVEL
Intermediate

MATERIALS
- Approximately 150 yds (137m) of fingering weight two-ply handspun yarn
- 1 set US #2 (2.75mm) double-pointed needles
- 1 US C-2 (2.75mm) crochet hook
- tapestry needle
- stitch markers

GAUGE (APPROXIMATE)
- In stockinette stitch
- 8 stitches and 12 rows = 1" (2.5cm)

SIZE
One size; approximately 7" (18cm) in length

Abbreviations & Techniques

k2tog Knit 2 stitches together.

psso Pass the slipped stitch over.

ssk (slip, slip, knit) This is a directional decrease. Individually slip the first two stitches from the left needle to the right, going into each stitch as if to knit. (You are putting a twist in the stitch.) Making sure that your working yarn is to the back of your work, take your left needle and insert the tip of that needle into the front of the two stitches that you just slipped to the right-hand needle. Now knit those two stitches together.

(continued on far right column)

DESIGNED BY LORI LAWSON OF CAPISTRANO FIBER ARTS

For this project, Lori spun a two-ply yarn using a Mount Rainier drop spindle from the Cascade Spindle Company. She used an extrafine merino/bombyx silk (50/50) roving that she handpainted. The color is "Barley," named after my dog! The yarn was spun in a fingering weight (approximately 15–16 wraps per inch [6 wraps per cm]). Each gauntlet is knit in the round on double-pointed needles.

lace pattern

The lace cuff uses the English Mesh Lace pattern from *A Treasury of Knitting Patterns* by Barbara G. Walker.

The lace pattern consists of a multiple of 6 stitches plus 1.

Rnd 1 and Odd-Numbered Rnds Knit.

Rnd 2 K1, *yo, ssk, k1, k2tog, yo, k1*; repeat from * to * to end of round.

Rnd 4 K1, *yo, k1, slip 1, k2tog, psso, k1, yo, k1*; repeat from * to * to end of round.

Rnd 6 K1, * k2tog, yo, k1, yo, ssk, k1*; repeat from * to * to end of round.

Rnd 8 K2tog, *(k1, yo) twice, k1, slip 1, k2tog, psso*; repeat from * to * to the last five stitches. End (k1, yo) twice, k1, ssk.

Note On Rnd 7, the knit row, Lori redistributed the stitches as she knit the round so that there were 20 stitches on needle 1, 18 stitches on needle 2, and 17 stitches on needle 3. This sets you up for an easier time knitting Rnd 8. Upon completion of Rnd 8, the stitches will be back to their original distribution of 19, 18, and 18.

Repeat Rnds 1 through 8.

instructions

Cast 55 stitches onto one double-pointed needle. Then divide these stitches onto three double-pointed needles, as follows: 19 stitches on needle 1, 18 stitches on needle 2, and 18 stitches on needle 3.

Be very careful not to twist your stitches when joining in the round. Use a locking stitch marker or the tail from the cast-on as a guide to mark the beginning of each round.

Rnd 1 Knit.

Rnds 2–33 Work the lace pattern.

Rnd 34 K2tog, then knit to the end of the round (54 sts).

Rnds 35–39 Work in garter stitch (purl 1 round, knit 1 round).

Rnds 40–57 Work in stockinette stitch (knit each round).

thumb opening

Rnd 1 Starting with needle 1, k4, bind off 10 sts, k3. (Needle 1 should have 4 stitches on either side of the thumb opening.) Continue in stockinette stitch on needles 2 and 3 to complete the round.

Rnd 2 Starting with needle 1, k4, cast on 10 sts, k4. (Needle 1 should have 18 sts.) Continue in stockinette stitch on needles 2 and 3 to complete the round.

Rnds 3–21 Work in stockinette stitch (knit each round).

Rnd 22 Purl.

crochet picot edge bind-off

With the crochet hook, chain 1 stitch into the stitch on the needle, then chain 3. Repeat this for every stitch on the needle. This will give a slightly ruffled effect.

Make the second gauntlet identical to the first.

finishing

Weave in the ends. Hand wash, then roll in a towel to remove excess water. Block and air dry for best results.

(continued from left column)

yo (yarn over) This is simply the act of bringing the yarn forward as if to purl, then following your pattern. For this pattern, after your yarn over, it calls for you to knit or ssk. So bring your yarn forward as if to purl, now you will either knit the first stitch on your left needle, or slip the first stitch from your left needle. You will notice that the working yarn comes back over the top of your needle from the front of your work. This is correct. It will create another stitch on your needle (an increase), and what looks like a hole in your work (the lacy open stitch).

ashford cold pad–dyed arm warmers

MATERIALS

- **Cashmere Arm Warmers knitted from pattern on page 52**
- **5¼ oz (150g) urea**
- **Rubbing alcohol**
- **1½ tsp (7.5mL) Polycell**
- **Dishwashing liquid (I used Dawn)**
- **Distilled white vinegar**
- **Ashford Wool Dye, color Teal**

TOOLS

- **Dust mask**
- **Gloves**
- **Measuring spoons**
- **Measuring cups**
- **Small whisks**
- **3 wide-mouth jars with lids, 2-cup (500mL) size**
- **3" (7.5cm) sponge brush**
- **Plastic wrap**

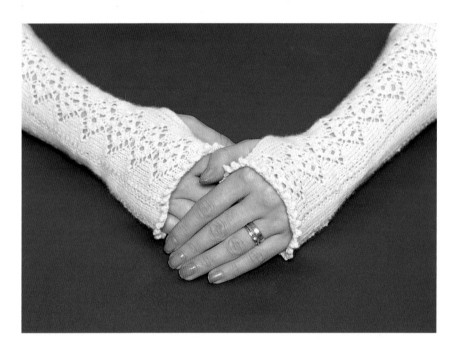

When it came to dyeing the Cashmere Arm Warmers, I have to say I was a little nervous at first. I was going to be taking a sponge brush to very expensive, very fine, and very soft knitted fabric. (Mitzi Good had provided me with a small sample that I was able to practice on.) I knew I didn't want to draw the brush across the fabric. Dabbing with the brush would be gentler and more effective, I hoped. The small sample held up just fine. My advice: If you are nervous, practice! You'll find that this technique is easy to do. Relax and have fun!

Note The padding mix should be made up 24 hours ahead of time. Sometimes the mix comes out lumpy, but if you let it sit overnight the lumps will disappear.

prepare the padding mixture

1. In a jar place 5¼ oz (150g) urea, pour in 1 cup (250mL) boiling water, and stir until dissolved. Add 1 cup (250mL) cold water.

2. Next add 1 tsp (5mL) rubbing alcohol and sprinkle 1½ tsp (7.5mL) Polycell into the mixture, stirring vigorously. Add 2 drops dishwashing liquid and 1 tbsp (15mL) vinegar; stir well.

3. Allow to sit overnight. After the padding mixture has cooled, keep it sealed until needed.

prepare the piece

4. Begin by soaking the arm warmers in a basin of warm water with 2 drops

dishwashing liquid for 1 hour. While the
arm warmers are soaking, mix up your
dyestock.

prepare the dye paste

5. Wearing your dust mask and gloves,
place ½ tsp (2.5g) dye powder in a jar,
add a little cold water, and mix well to
make a paste. Add 2 cups (500mL)
warm water and stir until the granules
dissolve. Set aside for at least 30
minutes to rest.

prepare the dyestock

6. Pour 1¼ cup (300mL) Padding
Mixture into the third jar, add 6 tbsp
(90mL) dyestock, and stir well.

paint the piece

7. Remove the arm warmers from the
soak solution and gently squeeze out
the excess water.

8. Place the pair of arm warmers side
by side on plastic wrap on your work
surface.

9. Using the 3" (7.5cm) sponge brush,
paint the entire surface of each arm
warmer with the mixture of padding
mixture and dyestock, being sure to
give good coverage. Turn the arm
warmers over and paint the other side.

10. Turn the arm warmers inside out and
repeat, paying attention to the seam—

be sure to cover this well. Once you
are satisfied with the coverage, seal the
arm warmers in plastic wrap and set
in a warm spot to cure. This can be a
sunny windowsill or near a radiator.
I left the sample arm warmers to cure
for 48 hours.

11. Soak the arm warmers in cold water
for 10 minutes, then very gently
(*no agitation*) wash the arm warmers in
warm water and dishwashing liquid 2-3
times. Rinse in warm water, gently
squeeze out excess water, and dry flat in
the shade. If you wish, you can block the
arm warmers out a bit so that the lace
pattern opens up.

STEP 8

STEP 9

STEP 10

cashmere arm warmers

DESIGNED BY MITZI GOOD AND LINDA LA BELLE

At the time I started to think about new patterns for the book, I asked my friend Takako Ueki of HABU Textiles what new yarn she might have to show me. Out came this lovely cashmere. So I took this yummy laceweight yarn to Mitzi Good and asked her what she envisioned knit up with this. "Lace arm warmers," she said! After many test swatches, here is what we came up with. The lace was inspired by lace stitches from Sharon Miller's book, *Heirloom Knitting*.

SKILL LEVEL
Advanced

MATERIALS
- A-34-1001 cashmere from HABU Textiles, 100% cashmere, 1 oz (28g), 404 yds (370m)
- 1 skein DMC Medicis Wool, color Ecru (to sew the seams)
- 1 set US #3 (3.25mm) straight needles
- 1 set US #4 (3.5mm) straight needles
- tapestry needle

GAUGE
- In stockinette stitch, on US #4 needles
- 30 stitches and 44 rows = 4" (10cm)

SIZE
One size; approximately 10.5" (27cm) in length

Abbreviations & Techniques
k2tog Knit 2 stitches together.

psso Pass the slipped stitch over.

How to sew an invisible seam
On the right side (outside) of the item, each stockinette stitch forms a "V," and at the base of the "V" is a horizontal bar, or ladder. Thread a tapestry needle with yarn and insert the needle under the bar on one side and then the other side, bar for bar. Pull just enough that the edges of the seam kiss—not too tight and not too loose. If done correctly, the seam is completely invisible.

suggestion

Knit both arm warmers at the same time. Divide yarn into two equal size and weight balls, and cast on for one arm warmer. With the second ball of yarn, cast on the second arm warmer on the same needle. Work across the first cast-on, then move all the stitches to the end of the right-hand needle. Continue with the second ball of yarn and second group of cast-on stitches.

instructions

Note The arm warmers are knit flat and then seamed together.

Using the US #4 needles, cast on 56 stitches.

Knit 9 rows in stockinette stitch, ending on a knit row.

Begin Lace pattern (Rows 1–13 on chart). Switch to the US #3 needles, and repeat Rows 2–13 seven more times (8 lace diamond pattern repeats).

Knit Row 14 on chart. Knit 3 rows in stockinette stitch, ending with a purl row.

picot edge

Using the US #4 needle, bind off 2 stitches. *Slip st on right needle to the left needle, cast on 2 sts, bind off 4 sts; repeat from *. Bind off 5 stitches.

Make the second arm warmer identical to the first, if making one at a time.

finishing

Note The cashmere is not suitably strong for sewing the seam; use the DMC Medicis Wool for seaming.

With wrong sides together, sew an invisible seam from the top of the arm warmer down 1½" (3.8cm). Leave a 2" (5cm) slit for the thumb, and then sew the remainder of the cuff. Weave in loose ends.

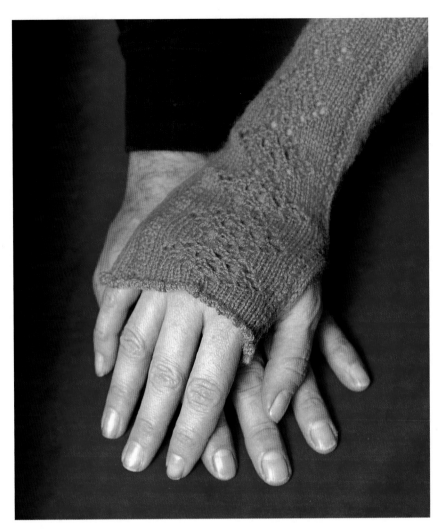

SIMPLE YARN SUBSTITUTION

If you don't want to dye the yarn but can't resist making a pair of these arm warmers, we found the perfect substitute. Frog Tree Alpaca Sport Weight, 100% alpaca, 1³/₄ oz (50g), 130 yds (119m). Keep everything the same except work on US #2 (2.75mm) and US #3 (3.25mm) needles.

- ⊙ & ☐ KNIT
- ⊟ PURL
- ⊘ KNIT 2 TOGETHER
- ◩ KNIT 2 TOGETHER
- ⊙ YARN OVER
- ▲ SLIP 1, KNIT 1, PASS THE
     SLIPPED STITCH OVER

kiton acid dyes

Most of the time I am not concerned about the dye leveling (dyeing the yarn evenly), but for certain projects I do feel it is important, and Kiton Acid Dyes are perfect for this.

The drawback to these dyes is that they are not 100 percent wash-fast. I happen to think this is a great dye on wool, for how often do we wash our woolens? And usually the washing is pretty gentle.

In this chapter, I've presented two different methods of immersion dyeing. Actually, the method is the same—just the ingredients change. For both of these projects, you will need to make your yarn into skeins—see instructions for making a skein on page 16.

For the leg warmers, I made stock with color straight from the jar, but for the hat I formulated a color. If you would like to formulate your own color, start with several stock colors. Have some small containers ready in which to blend colors together, keeping notes. Test these new colors on a white coffee filter. When you have a mixture you like, mix up a quantity of it. That's what I did to find the rich green for the hat (page 60).

kiton immersion–dyed merino wool

MATERIALS

- **4 balls of Treliske Organic Merino Wool, 100% wool, 1 3/4 oz (50g), 110 yds (100m) each, made into 60" (152cm) skeins, color Marle**
- **Synthrapol**
- **Kiton Acid Dye, color National Blue CK445**
- **Noniodized salt**
- **Citric acid crystals**

TOOLS

- **Dust mask**
- **Gloves**
- **Measuring spoons**
- **Measuring cups**
- **1 wide-mouth jar with lid, 2-cup size (500mL)**
- **Small whisks**
- **Plastic ladle**
- **Stainless steel or enamel pot**

I usually dye the Treliske yarn we used in this project with indigo, a natural dye. But I tested the blues from Kiton and found that National Blue CK445 gave me the same sense of indigo blue.

prepare the yarn

1. Begin by soaking the skeins in a bowl of warm water and 1/2 tsp (2.5mL) of Synthrapol for 1 hour. While your yarn is soaking, mix your color.

prepare the dyestock

2. Wearing your gloves and dust mask, place 1/2 tsp (2.5g) of dye powder in a glass measuring cup, add a small amount of warm water, and stir into a paste. Add 7 fl. oz (200mL) of boiling water, stir thoroughly, and set aside to rest for 1 hour.

3. In a stainless steel or enamel pot place 6 qt (6L) water at approximately 85°F

(30°C). The pot should be large enough for the yarn to move freely. Add your dye solution, 1 1/2 tbsp (20g) salt, 1 tsp (5mL) Synthrapol, and 1 tbsp (15mL) citric acid. Stir thoroughly.

add the yarn

4. Remove the yarn from the soak solution, gently squeeze out any excess water, and add the yarn to the dyepot. Carefully stir the yarn in the pot by gently turning the yarn over for about 3-5 minutes to distribute the dye uniformly.

5. Slowly raise the temperature to just below a boil, 195°F (90°C). Set your timer for 60 minutes and maintain this temperature, stirring periodically. The dyepot should be exhausted. If the dyebath does not completely exhaust, I suggest you add 1/4 to 1/2 cup (60-120mL) distilled white vinegar and maintain the temperature for another 15 minutes.

STEP 4

6. Allow the dyebath to cool completely—this is important because the color is still changing as the dyebath cools down.

remove the yarn

7. Remove the yarn and rinse gently in warm water. Squeeze out any excess water and allow to air dry.

8. Once the skeins are dry, stretch them back out under tension and wind into balls.

STEP 4 (CONTINUED)

STEP 5

cabled leg warmers

Abbreviations & Techniques

C4F (cable 4 front) Slip 2 stitches to the cable needle and hold at the front of your work. Knit the next 2 stitches on your left needle. Now knit the 2 stitches from the cable needle, being sure not to twist your stitches as you do so.

(continued on right column)

DESIGNED BY LAURA COOPER AND LINDA LA BELLE

Laura Cooper came to my shop to learn to knit. She is a knitwear designer for a fashion house here in New York City. In school in England, she learned to machine knit and design knitwear but had never learned to handknit. Having taken several sessions at the shop, she wanted to try her hand at cables. Knowing she could handle a challenge, I asked her to come up with something for the book.

instructions

Note The leg warmers are knit from the top down.

Using the US #6 needles, cast on 78 stitches. Transfer these stitches to the US #3 circular needle, being sure to slip the stitches as if to purl so that they are not facing the wrong direction when you begin to knit. Join, being careful the cast-on is not twisted.

Note It's important that you cast on and bind off on larger needles for this project. The cast-on and bind-off get the most stress when the legwarmers are being put on and taken off, and you want these parts to be stretchy but sturdy.

Work in k1, p1 ribbing for 2¼" (5.5cm).

Switch to the US #4 circular needle and work 1 round in stockinette stitch (knit each round). Working 1 round in stockinette stitch before and after the chart produces a smoother transition into and out of the cable pattern.

Work three repeats of the chart on page 59 (rounds 1 through 24), for a total of 72 pattern rounds.

Switch to the US #3 circular needle and work one more repeat of the chart.

Next, work 1 round in stockinette stitch (knit each round).

Still on the US #3 circular needle, work in k1, p1 ribbing for 1½" (3.8cm).

Bind off in the ribbing pattern using the US #6 needles.

Weave in the ends.

(continued from left column)

C4B (cable 4 back) Slip 2 stitches to the cable needle and hold at the back of your work. Knit the 2 stitches on your left needle. Now knit the 2 stitches from the cable needle, being sure not to twist your stitches as you do so.

C8B (cable 8 back) Slip 4 stitches to the cable needle and hold at the back of your work. Knit the next 4 stitches on your left needle. Now knit the 4 stitches from the cable needle, being sure not to twist your stitches as you do so.

SIMPLE YARN SUBSTITUTION

If you fell in love with the Cabled Leg Warmers but you do not wish to dye the yarn, I found the perfect substitution yarn. It is New England Highland from Harrisville Designs, Inc., 4 oz (113.5g), 200 yds (183m). We were able to keep the same needle size and match the gauge. The sample swatch is knit

☐ KNIT
⊡ PURL
◣◣◣◣ C4F
◥◥◥◥ C4B
◤◤◤◤◤◤◤◤ C8B

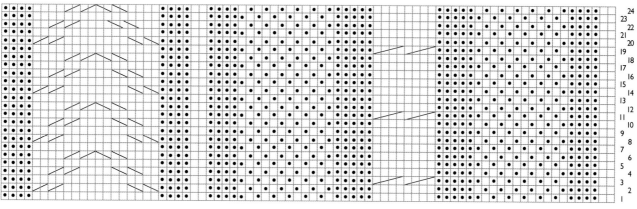

kiton immersion–dyed alpaca and silk/mohair

MATERIALS

- **1 ball Frog Tree 100% Alpaca Sport Weight, 1³/₄ oz (50g), 130 yds (118m) each**
- **1 skein HABU Textiles A32B Silk/Mohair, ¹/₂ oz (14g), 187 yds (170m)**
- **Synthrapol**
- **Kiton Acid Dye in the following colors: Yellow, National Blue CK445, Bright Blue**
- **Noniodized salt**
- **Distilled white vinegar**

TOOLS

- **Dust mask**
- **Gloves**
- **Measuring spoons**
- **Measuring cups**
- **4 wide-mouth jars with lids, 2-cup size (500mL)**
- **Small whisks**
- **Plastic ladle**
- **Stainless steel or enamel pot**
- **Candy thermometer**

For the Beaded Hat (page 62), I wanted to try mixing different substrates, so I used a 100 percent alpaca yarn with a silk/mohair blend. The outcome was that the alpaca took the dye as did the mohair in the blend, but the silk did not. This gave me a lovely yarn with highlights that are then picked up by the beads.

The color itself was suggested by Mitzi Good; she was looking at a felted piece on the wall of my studio and asked if I could make a similar green.

Note When you wind your skein for the hat, run both the alpaca and the silk/mohair together, so that you are dyeing one skein.

prepare the yarn

1. Rewind both yarns together into one 60" (150cm) skein.

2. In a basin, soak the skein in warm water with ¹/₂ tsp (2.5mL) Synthrapol for 1 hour. While your yarn is soaking, mix your color.

prepare the dyestock

3. Wearing gloves and a dust mask, place ¹/₄ tsp (1g) of each color dye powder in each of three wide-mouth jars that have been labeled with the color names. Add a small amount of warm water to each jar and stir into a paste. Add 3¹/₂ oz (100mL) boiling water to each jar, stir thoroughly, and set aside to rest for 1 hour.

4. Make a salt solution by mixing ¹/₃ oz (10g) of noniodized salt with 3¹/₂ fl. oz (100mL) boiling water. Set aside to cool. Next, you will mix into your fourth wide-mouth jar the following dyestock: Yellow 2¹/₂ fl. oz (74mL); National Blue 1¹/₂ fl. oz (44mL); Bright Blue 1 fl. oz (30mL). Stir well.

5. In a stainless steel or enamel pot, place 5 quarts (5L) water at approximately 85°F (30°C). The pot should be large enough for the yarn to move freely. Add your green dyestock, 1 tbsp (15mL) salt solution, 1 tsp (5mL) Synthrapol, and 4 fl. oz (132mL) vinegar. Stir thoroughly.

STEP 6

STEP 6 (CONTINUED)

STEP 7

add the yarn

6. Remove the yarn from the soak solution, gently squeeze out any excess water, and add to the dyepot. Carefully stir the dyepot, turning the yarn over for about 3-5 minutes to distribute the dye uniformly.

7. Slowly raise the temperature to just below a boil, 195°F (90°C). Maintain this temperature for 60 minutes, stirring periodically. The dyepot should be exhausted. If the dyebath does not completely exhaust, I suggest that you add ¼ to ½ cup (60-120mL) vinegar while holding the yarn out of the way and maintain the temperature for another 15 minutes.

8. Allow the dyebath to cool completely—this is important because the color is still changing as the dyebath cools down.

remove the yarn

9. Remove the yarn and rinse gently in warm water. Squeeze out any excess water and allow to air dry.

10. Once the skeins are dry, stretch them back out under tension and wind into balls.

beaded hat

DESIGNED BY DONNA FISCINA AND LINDA LA BELLE

Donna has taken many classes at The Yarn Tree—not just knitting, but weaving, felting, and spinning, too. When I was first thinking about patterns for this book, Donna was taking a knitting class from me. She wanted me to tell her what to do for her next project, but I decided that it was time for Donna to learn how to design something of her own. It took Donna several swatches, but her hard work paid off, and she came up with this great hat. She was inspired by the Tutti Twists cable in Nicky Epstein's *Knitting on the Edge: Ribs, Ruffles, Lace, Fringes, Floral, Points & Picot: The Essential Collection of 350 Decorative Borders*. Congratulations, Donna!

instructions

Note The band for this hat is knit first, joined, and then you pick up stitches and knit in the round for the top of the hat.

Cast on 20 sts, using the provisional cast-on method.

Row 1 (RS) Knit.

Row 2 (WS) K1, p1, k1, [p1, k2] twice, p2, [k2, p1] twice, p3.

Row 3 K3, [1/1 LPC, p1] twice, k2, [p1, 1/1 RPC] twice, k1, p1, k1.

Row 4 K1, p1, k2, p1, k2, p1, k1, p2, k1, p1, k2, p1, k1, p3.

Row 5 K3, [p1, 1/1 LPC] twice, k2, [1/1 RPC, p1] twice, k1, p1, k1.

Row 6 K1, p1, k3, p1, k2, p4, k2, p1, k2, P3.

Row 7 K3, p2, 1/1 LPC, p1, k4, p1, 1/1 RPC, p2, k1, p1, k1.

Row 8 K1, p1, k4, p1, k1, p4, k1, p1, k3, p3.

Row 9 K3, p3, 1/1 LPC, k4, 1/1 RPC, p3, k1, p1, k1.

Row 10 K1, p1, k5, p6, k4, p3.

Row 11 K3, p4, 6 St RC, p4, k1, p1, k1.

Row 12 K1, p1, k5, p6, k4, p3.

Row 13 K3, p3, 1/1 RPC, k4, 1/1 LPC, p3, k1, p1, k1.

Row 14 K1, p1, k4, p1, k1, p4, k1, p1, k3, p3.

Row 15 K3, p2, 1/1 RPC, p1, k4, p1, 1/1 LPC, p2, k1, p1, k1.

Row 16 K1, p1, k3, p1, k2, p4, k2, p1, k2, p3.

Row 17 K3, [p1, 1/1 RPC] twice, k2, [1/1 LPC, p1] twice, k1, p1, k1.

Row 18 K1, p1, k2, p1, k2, p1, k1, p2, k1, p1, k2, p1, k1, p3.

SKILL LEVEL
Intermediate to Advanced

MATERIALS
- 1 ball Frog Tree 100% Alpaca Sport Weight, 1³/₄ oz (50g), 130 yds (118m)
- HABU Textiles #A-32B Silk/Mohair, 60% silk, 40% mohair, ¹/₂ oz (14g), 185 yds (169m)
- 180 4mm beads
- 1 pair US #4 (3.5mm) straight needles
- 1 16" (40.5cm) US #4 (3.5mm) circular needle
- 1 set US #4 (3.5mm) double-pointed needles
- cable needle
- tapestry needle

GAUGE
- In stockinette stitch
- 20 stitches and 32 rows = 4" (10cm)

SIZE
To fit a 21" (53cm) head

Abbreviations & Techniques

1/1 LPC Slip one stitch to a cable needle (without twisting), and hold to the front of your work. Purl 1, then knit the stitch from the cable needle.

1/1 RPC Slip one stitch to a cable needle (without twisting), and hold to the back of your work. Knit 1, then purl the stitch from the cable needle.

(continued on page 64)

(continued from page 62)

6 St RC Slip 3 stitches to a cable needle (without twisting), and hold in back of your work. Knit 3, then knit the 3 stitches from the cable needle.

k2tog Knit 2 stitches together.

knit pick up Insert the tip of the right-hand needle under the edge stitch, wrap the yarn, and pull the loop through.

provisional cast-on This cast-on is used when you need live stitches for grafting later. Begin with a yard of waste yarn in a contrasting color that is close to the thickness of the project yarn.

Matching the end of the waste yarn with the end of your working yarn, tie an overhand knot about 2" (5cm) from the cut ends. Place one of your needles against the knot, and hold the knot in place against the needle with your right thumb. The two yarns will be placed in your left hand as follows: The working yarn should be to the right of and going over the needle, then it wraps your left index finger from left to right and rests in the palm of your hand. The waste yarn wraps around the inside of your thumb and back to your palm with the yarn resting in the palm of your hand. Hold the two tails in place with your free fingers. You have formed a "V" from your thumb and index finger to the needle. Insert the needle into the loop of waste yarn around your thumb from underneath.

Bring the needle over the loop around your index finger and down into that loop, catching the working yarn. Bring the working yarn on your needle down through the loop of waste yarn on your thumb. Remove the waste yarn from your thumb and adjust the tension of the loop on your needle.

Place your thumb against the waste yarn and begin again. Repeat until you have the desired number of stitches.

When you are ready to graft or pick up these stitches, carefully snip the waste yarn and place the live stitches on a needle.

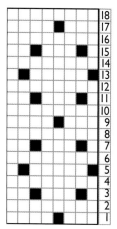

REPEAT 12X

☐ KNIT
■ BEADING STITCH

Row 19 K3, [1/1 RPC, p1] twice, k2, [p1, 1/1 LPC] twice, k1, p1, k1.

Repeat Rows 2 through 19 seven more times.

Next Row Purl. Using Kitchener stitch, join the cast-on edge to the working stitches to form a ring.

top of hat

String 180 beads onto the yarn. Slide the beads down the yarn until you need them. With beaded yarn and the circular needle, knit pick up 104 stitches around the band.

Rnd 1 Join and decrease as follows: *k24, k2tog*; repeat from * to * 3 more times (100 sts).

Rnd 2 Knit.

Rnd 3 Decrease as follows: *k23, k2tog*; repeat from * to * 3 more times (96 sts).

Following the chart for the next 18 rounds, incorporate the beads as follows:

Knit to beading stitch. Bring yarn to front and slip beading stitch to right needle. Slide bead to sit in front of slipped stitch, then bring yarn to back. Knit to next beading stitch. This technique places the beads in front of the slipped stitch, ensuring that the beads won't slip to the wrong side.

Rnd 22 *K14, k2tog*; repeat from * to * 6 times (90 sts).

Rnd 23 Knit.

Rnd 24 *K13, k2tog*; repeat from * to * 6 times (84 sts).

Rnd 25 Knit.

Rnd 26 *K12, k2tog*; repeat from * to * 6 times (78 sts).

Rnd 27 Knit.

Rnd 28 *K11, k2tog*; repeat from * to * 6 times (72 sts).

Rnd 29 Knit.

Rnd 30 *K10, k2tog*; repeat from * to * 6 times (66 sts).

Rnd 31 Knit.

Rnd 32 *K9, k2tog*; repeat from * to * 6 times (60 sts).

Rnd 33 Knit.

Rnd 34 *K8, k2tog*; repeat from * to * 6 times (54 sts).

Rnd 35 Knit.

Rnd 36 *K7, k2tog*; repeat from * to * 6 times (48 sts).

Switch to double-pointed needles.

Rnd 37 *K6, k2tog*; repeat from * to * 6 times (42 sts).

Rnd 38 *K5, k2tog*; repeat from * to * 6 times (36 sts).

Rnd 39 *K4, k2tog*; repeat from * to * 6 times (30 sts).

Rnd 40 *K3, k2tog*; repeat from * to * 6 times (24 sts).

Rnd 41 *K2, k2tog*; repeat from * to * 6 times (18 sts).

Rnd 42 *K1, k2tog*; repeat from * to * 6 times (12 sts).

Cut a long tail, thread a tapestry needle, and slip the stitches from the knitting needle onto the tapestry needle down onto the yarn. When all the stitches are off the knitting needle, pull tight on the yarn to close, and weave in the ends.

SIMPLE YARN SUBSTITUTION

If you fell in love with the Beaded Hat, but you do not wish to dye the yarn, you can substitute the already dyed manufacturer's yarn. Here we knit a sample swatch in Frog Tree's 100% Alpaca Sport Weight, 1³/₄ oz (50g), 130 yds (118m), color #25 and HABU Textile's A-32B Silk/ Mohair, 60% silk, 40% mohair, ¹/₂ oz (14g), 185 yds (169m), color #6. We were able to keep the same needle size and match the gauge.

kitchener stitch The Kitchener stitch is used to join live stitches; the seam looks like a continuous row of stockinette stitch. It's important that you match the tension of the work—you do not want your seam to be too loose nor too tight.

Place the live stitches on two needles evenly. Cut the working yarn approximately four times the width of the work. Thread a tapestry needle with the working yarn. Hold the two needles together in your left hand, with the right side (knit side) of the work facing out. (Note: It does not matter if the working yarn is on the front needle or the back needle.)

Bring the working yarn through the first stitch on the front needle, going into the stitch as if to purl. Leave this stitch on the needle. Next, bring the working yarn through the first stitch on the back needle as if to knit, and leave that stitch on the needle.

Step 1 Bring the working yarn through the first stitch on the front needle as if to knit, and slip that stitch off the needle.

Step 2 Bring the working yarn through the next stitch on the front needle as if to purl and leave this stitch on the needle.

(Here it gets a little tricky. When going from the front needle to the back needle, be sure that the working yarn does not end up **over** the front needle—this will become a yarn over and add a stitch, making a hole! The working yarn should come under the front needle and up between the two needles.)

Step 3 Bring the working yarn through the first stitch on the back needle as if to purl, and slip that stitch off the needle.

Step 4 Bring the working yarn through the first stitch on the back needle as if to knit, and leave this stitch on the needle. (It is at this point that you can count the stitches— you should have the same number on both needles!)

Repeat these four steps until you have one stitch remaining on each needle, and then follow steps 1 and 3.

NANCY FINN, CHASING RAINBOWS DYEWORKS

I met Nancy Finn several years ago at the Dutchess County Sheep and Wool Festival in Rhinebeck, New York. When I saw the beautiful color palette on display in her booth, I just had to ask if she would sell wholesale to my shop. Happily, her answer was yes!

I was eager to visit Nancy at her studio in Willits, California, and get to know her outside the chaos of a craft fair atmosphere. On a beautiful sunny day in August, after my visit with Darlene Hayes (page 32), I jumped in my rental car and made the drive up north. To get to her studio, I drove through miles and miles of agricultural land (it was tomato season) and then climbed into the mountains on a winding road.

I met Nancy at Chasing Rainbows, where we went outside to talk, sitting down on bales of hay under a stand of madrona trees with birds chirping in the background. Nancy's career in dyeing started when she dyed feathers for a commission, using Rit dye on her stovetop—the color turned out perfect. (Later she would learn about "real" dyes.) After her move to Willits from the San Francisco Bay area with her husband, Dave, Nancy went to the local junior college to learn to spin. Her original thought had been to raise sheep, dye their wool, spin it into yarn, and knit the yarn into finished goods. She quickly realized how much work that would be. Instead, she could simply buy the wool from the large number of sheep farms in the area at that time and have it prepared into yarn or roving that she could then dye.

She began a business. At craft fairs, she sold knitted garments from yarns she had spun and dyed. At one of these fairs, a twelve-year-old girl spotted some of Nancy's hand-dyed roving and wanted to buy it. Nancy asked the girl what she was going to do with it. Her reply: "I just want to look at it." This caused a lightbulb to go off in Nancy's head: Why not just sell the roving or yarns? To heck with the finished goods!

By the late 1980s, she was taking her hand-dyed yarns to weavers' conferences and knitting shows. That's how Chasing Rainbows Dyeworks, as we know it today, began.

Chasing Rainbows Dyeworks sits on a hilltop surrounded by 18 acres of trees and quite a bit of poison oak (which I managed to avoid!). There is a barn for the three alpacas, Smokey the dog, and several cats. Nancy's operation has moved from her kitchen to its own building, which houses the dye studio, storage, and office space. Dave oversaw the work on the building. There are lots of windows and even a deck that overlooks Nancy's garden.

Nancy no longer works alone, but has several employees. I met two of them. Theresa Moore has been with Nancy for eight years and is now training Alana Lopes. The day I was there, Alana had graduated from dyeing roving to dyeing yarn.

When Nancy began to dye in earnest, Dave's great-grandmother's quilt was her main color inspiration. She told me she would spend hours looking at the color combinations in this quilt, made from dressmaker's scraps. Those original color combos are still in her line today.

Nancy enjoys all the steps of this labor-intensive business, finding that if she gets bored with one she can go on to the next. Her advice to someone starting out is that you had better love

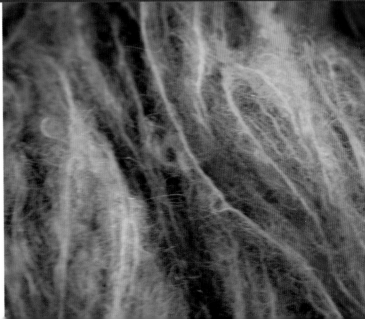

every step. Start out slowly. Dye the yarn or roving and then be sure to take it through to the end—spin the roving and knit the yarn. This is the only way you can really see how the dyes work out.

In addition to her work at shows, she also gives color workshops that employ the use of the color wheel. She is a knitter, weaver, spinner, and dyer, but unfortunately as a businesswoman she has little time to do any of these. She will occasionally custom dye for select clients, which gives her a welcome break from the day-to-day routine.

When Nancy was studying spinning, she dabbled a little bit with natural dyes, but her business has focused solely on chemical dyes. She is making plans to go to Oaxaca, Mexico, a center of weaving and natural dyeing in southern Mexico, to study natural dyeing.

Here is a secret she shared with me: When you are dyeing yarn or roving, it is about color—proportion and balance of color. If you have equal amounts of color it will cause people to turn away, but if you have more of a dominant color and less of a highlight color, your yarn or roving will be more interesting and will draw people in.

"Start out slowly, and love every step."

THIS PAGE, CLOCKWISE FROM TOP: Theresa Moore instructs Alana Lopes in the art of dyeing yarn. Bottles of prepared dyestock at the ready. Nancy Finn in her studio. Dave's grandmother's quilt, which had such a strong influence on Nancy's color choices for her yarns. Jesse, one of three alpacas at Chasing Rainbows, basking in the sun. OPPOSITE PAGE, LEFT TO RIGHT: Alana pours prepared dyestock onto wool roving. One of the many beautiful yarns from Chasing Rainbows, Brushed Mohair comes in these two luscious colorways plus plenty more.

jacquard acid dyes

The versatility and ease of use is really what got me hooked on Jacquard Acid dyes. All you need is hot water and distilled white vinegar, and with forty vibrant colors to work with, you will never run out of color choices.

For this chapter I used the dyes with several different substrates: mohair, alpaca, and silk. I did immersion dyeing, handpainting, a soak technique, and a microwave technique. I am sure you will enjoy the following projects as much as I did!

jacquard immersion-dyed silk

MATERIALS

- **3 skeins Spun Silk NM 5/2 from Henry's Attic, 100% silk, 3½ oz (100g), 273 yds (250m)**
- **Jacquard Acid Dyes in the following colors: 627 Kelly Green, 621 Sky Blue, 629 Emerald**
- **Distilled white vinegar**
- **Synthrapol**

TOOLS

- **Dust mask**
- **Gloves**
- **Enamel or stainless steel pot**
- **Candy thermometer**
- **Measuring spoons**
- **Measuring cups**
- **Small whisks**
- **3 small jars in which to mix dyestock**
- **1 medium container for the final color**
- **Large plastic or stainless steel spoon for stirring the dyepot**

For this project, I choose Henry's Attic Spun Silk NM 5/2. Before dyeing, I worked with Yvette Byas, my crochet instructor, to come up with a structure for a crochet shawl (page 72) that would have lots of lovely drape and would also be able to support the crochet flowers that I had in mind (see page 102).

After making several swatches, we settled on one. Then we talked about the length and width of the shawl. Because I had chosen a more open crochet structure, I began to see this shawl as a very spring/summer piece.

So into the dye studio I went, with the idea of a soft summer green in my head. I find the Jacquard Acid Dye very easy to use and mix into color formulas when made into dyestock. If you would like to formulate your own color, start with several stock colors. Have some small containers ready in which to blend colors together, keeping notes. Test these new colors on a white coffee filter. When you have a mixture you like, mix up a quantity of it. That's what I did to find my Summer Green!

prepare the dyestock

1. Be sure to wear your dust mask and gloves. In individual containers labeled with the color names, combine a small amount of very warm water with the dye to form a paste. Once it is smooth, add the remaining warm water to equal the amounts below.

   Kelly Green: 1 tsp dye (5g) powder to 7 fl. oz (215mL) water

   Sky Blue: ½ tsp (2.5mL) dyestock to 5 fl. oz (155mL) water

   Emerald: ½ tsp (2mL) dyestock to 5 fl. oz (155mL) water

2. Set these jars of color aside to rest for at least 1 hour.

prepare the yarn

3. While your dyestock is resting, soak your silk in a dishpan with ½ tsp (2.5mL) Synthrapol, ¼ cup (60mL) vinegar, and warm water to cover.

STEP 6

STEP 7

STEP 8

prepare the dyepot

4. Mix the following amounts of dyestock together to make the Summer Green dyestock: 6 fl. oz (185mL) + 2 tsp (10mL) Kelly Green, 1 fl. oz (30mL) Sky Blue, 1 fl. oz (30mL) Emerald

5. Place 7 qt (7L) of water and the Summer Green dyestock in the pot and stir well.

add the yarn

6. Place your yarn in the pot, turning over gently and ensuring all the yarn is submerged.

7. Slowly bring the pot up to 185°F (85°C). Add 1/2 cup + 3 tbsp (165mL) vinegar using one of two methods:

Remove the yarn from the pot completely, reintroducing it after adding the vinegar; or hold the yarn to one side of the pot and carefully pour in the vinegar, being sure not to get the vinegar on the yarn directly. Stir and submerge the yarn again. Maintain this temperature for 30 minutes. If the dyebath has not exhausted by this time, add another dose of vinegar and continue at the same temperature.

8. Once the dyebath has exhausted or nearly exhausted, allow the yarn to cool completely in the pot (this will take several hours). This is very important. You will get better color and better adherence of the dyestuff if you wait.

remove the yarn

9. Remove the yarn from the pot and rinse in warm water with 1/4 tsp (1.25mL) Synthrapol, then rinse in clear water 2-3 times. Allow the yarn to air dry.

10. Once the skeins are dry, stretch them back out under tension and wind into balls.

Note If, in the end, you find that you have leftover dyestock, you can store it covered and it will remain stable for quite a long time, although you may need to warm the dyestock to get the colors to mix well. To warm the dyestock, place the container in a pan of hot water.

crochet shawl

SKILL LEVEL
Beginner

MATERIALS
- **3 skeins Spun Silk NM 5/2 from Henry's Attic, 100% silk, 3¹/₂ oz (100g), 273 yds (250m) each**

- **1 US G-6 (4mm) crochet hook**

- **tapestry needle**

GAUGE
- **16 double crochet = 4" (10cm)**

SIZE
19" (48.5cm) wide by 65" (165cm) long after blocking

Abbreviations

ch chain

dc double crochet

sl st slip stitch

DESIGNED BY YVETTE BYAS AND LINDA LA BELLE

Yvette's inspiration for this shawl came from the Large Mesh Ground pattern in Berry Barden's *The Crochet Stitch Bible.*

instructions

Ch 107.

Row 1 Work 1 dc in the 8th ch from hook, *ch 2, skip 2 ch, 1 dc in the next ch*; repeat from * to * to the end, turn.

Row 2 Ch 5, skip the first dc and ch 2, *1 dc in the next dc, ch 2, skip 2 ch*; repeat from * to *; ending 1 dc in the next ch, turn.

Repeat Row 2 106 times.

edging

Keeping the shawl flat, *3 dc in any corner and 1 dc in each space until you reach the next corner*; repeat from * to * around the shawl (always doing 3 dc in the corners). Ch 1, and join to 1st dc, fasten off.

finishing

Weave in the ends.

Block your shawl by soaking it in warm water for 10 minutes. Roll it up in a towel to remove excess water. Lay flat on a dry towel and, using a tape measure, gently shape the shawl into a rectangle measuring 19" (48.5cm) by 65" (165cm). Allow to dry flat. After the shawl is dry, attach the flowers (page 102).

jacquard microwave–dyed mohair

MATERIALS

- **1 Ball Joseph Galler Flore II, 75% kid mohair/15% wool/10% nylon, 1³/₄ oz (50g), 100 yds (109m), Hot Pink Color #063**
- **Distilled white vinegar**
- **Synthrapol**
- **Jacquard Acid Dye, Jet Black #639**

TOOLS

- **Measuring spoons**
- **Measuring cups**
- **Dust mask**
- **Gloves**
- **Container to hold the dyestock**
- **Microwave-safe dish**
- **Plastic wrap**
- **Syringe**

What if you had one ball of yarn left over after finishing a project and you wanted to use it up, but you were a little tired of the color? Here is a great way to change it slightly, making a speckled skein. Use it to crochet up a scarf (page 76).

prepare the yarn

1. Make the yarn into a 60-inch (152.5cm) skein, following the how-to on page 16.

2. Soak the yarn in enough warm water to cover with ¹/₄ cup (60mL) vinegar and ¹/₄ tsp (1.25mL) Synthrapol. Allow the yarn to soak for at least 1 hour.

prepare the dyestock

3. Wearing your dust mask and gloves, make a paste of 1 tsp (5g) dye powder and 1 fl. oz (30mL) water. When smooth, add 2 fl. oz (60mL) more water. This will give you a very strong black dyestock perfect for overdyeing yarn.

4. Allow the dyestock to sit for at least 1 hour.

paint the yarn

5. Mix a water-vinegar solution of ¹/₄ cup (60mL) vinegar and ³/₄ cup (180mL) water and set aside.

6. Remove the skein of yarn from the water and gently squeeze it out—or use a salad spinner to get out the excess water. Place the yarn in the microwavable container by spiraling it around itself.

7. Pour in enough water-vinegar solution to just cover the yarn.

8. Using the syringe, take up some dyestock. Following the spiral of the yarn, place the syringe on the yarn and gently squeeze a small amount of the stock onto the yarn. You can also position the syringe between and more deeply into the strands of yarn and gently squeeze.

STEP 6

STEP 6 (CONTINUED)

STEP 7

STEP 8

STEP 10

STEP 10 (CONTINUED)

9. Continue squirting small dots of dye onto the yarn, refilling the syringe as needed until you have the amount of black speckles that you want. Be careful not to get carried away with the syringe—a little dye goes a long way! Note that as you are doing this, some of the dyestock will settle on the bottom of the container.

microwave the yarn

10. Cover the container with plastic wrap—I like to put a piece in one direction and a second piece in the other direction.

Without disturbing the contents of the bowl too much, place the container in the microwave.

11. Microwave on high for 3 minutes, and then let it sit for 3 minutes. Repeat this process two more times for a total microwaving time of 9 minutes. Please note that if you attempt to microwave for 9 minutes straight with no break in between, there is a very strong chance that your yarn will burn—please don't do it!

12. Allow the yarn to cool completely before removing the plastic wrap. There

are two reasons for this: It is too hot and you may burn yourself, and the color take-up on the yarn will be better if you allow the yarn to cool before washing.

13. Remove the plastic wrap and soak the yarn in warm water and ¼ tsp (1.25mL) of Synthrapol for about 5 minutes. Gently rinse the yarn 3–4 times in warm water. Do *not* agitate the yarn. Allow the yarn to air dry.

14. Once the yarn is dry, stretch the skein back out under tension and wind into a ball.

rock 'n' roll scarf

DESIGNED BY YVETTE BYAS

The yarn for this scarf, Flore II from Joseph Galler, comes in a wide range of colors, so don't just stop with Hot Pink!

SKILL LEVEL
Beginner

MATERIALS
- 1 ball Joseph Galler Flore II 75% kid mohair/15% wool/ 10% nylon, 1³/₄ oz (50g), 100 yds (109m), Hot Pink Color #063

- 1 US P-16 (11.5mm) crochet hook

- tapestry needle

GAUGE
- 5 treble crochet = 3¹/₂" (8.9cm)

SIZE
Approximately 3" (7.5cm) wide by 60" (152.5cm) long

instructions

Ch 12.

Row 1 Tr in fifth ch from hook, ch 1, skip 1 ch, tr in the next ch, *ch 1, skip 1 ch, tr in the next ch*; repeat from * to * to end.

Row 2 Ch 5 (counts as tr and 1 ch), tr in the first ch space, *ch 1, tr in the next ch 1 space*; repeat from * to * to end.

Repeat Row 2 until scarf measures 55" (139.5cm).

Weave in the ends.

fringe

With the remaining yarn, cut 24 strands of yarn 20" (51cm) long. Make eight groups of three, and fold these pieces in half. With your crochet hook, draw the loop through the space on the bottom edge of your scarf and pull the tails through the loop. Continue in this manner, placing four groups on each end of the scarf.

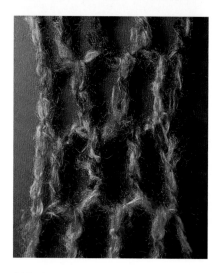

Abbreviations

ch chain stitch

tr treble crochet

jacquard soak–dyed alpaca

MATERIALS

- **2 balls Frog Tree 100% Alpaca Chunky, 100% alpaca, 1³⁄₄ oz (50g), 54 yds (49m)**
- **Acrylic yarn in at least two different colors**
- **Jacquard Acid Dyes in the following colors: #604 Burnt Orange, #605 Pumpkin Orange, #606 Deep Orange, #611 Vermillion, #617 Cherry Red**
- **Distilled white vinegar**
- **Synthrapol**

TOOLS

- **Dust mask**
- **Gloves**
- **Enamel or stainless steel pot**
- **Measuring spoons**
- **Measuring cups**
- **Small whisks**
- **Plastic wrap**
- **5 medium containers in which to mix dyestock, labeled with the color name or number of the dyes**
- **5 wide-mouth mason jars, 2-cup size (500mL), also marked with the color name or number of the dyes**
- **Vegetable steamer**

It was the night of July 4, and I was flying out the next day to do an interview, but I wanted to get some yarn dyed before I left. The streets of my neighborhood were filled with people coming to watch the fireworks along the waterfront, the weather was terribly hot, and I was looking for inspiration. It was all around me. I wanted the yarn to reflect the heat and excitement that was just outside my studio, so I chose a yellow yarn and red and orange dyes to make Fireworks Yarn. This is a simple technique that shows how you can overdye yarn.

I want to thank Dana Vessa, who took a Kool-Aid dyeing workshop from me and asked a "what if" question that led me to first try this technique.

prepare the yarn

1. Begin by making two skeins that are 8 yds (7.3m) long. Make the first skein, but do not remove it. Now make the second skein so that you are stacking the skeins one above the other, being sure that the starting and ending points match up.

This helps ensure that the two skeins are dyed in such a way that when you knit up the Half Mitts the yarn will match. Because of the length of the skein that you are making, you will run out of yarn before you get back to the beginning to tie the two ends together. To solve this problem, tie on some acrylic yarn and use that to get back to the beginning; tie the two ends together.

2. Starting at either end of each skein, make figure 8s using the first color of acrylic yarn. Using the second color of acrylic yarn, place figure 8s along each skein. Next, place figure 8s through both skeins. This will help to hold them together. Make several larkshead knots along the length of the skein, going around both sides. This will keep it tidy while the skein is soaking.

3. Soak the yarn in a dishpan with ¹⁄₂ tsp (2.5mL) Synthrapol, ¹⁄₄ cup (60mL) vinegar, and warm water to cover for 1 hour.

prepare the dyestock

4. Mix each color up individually in the five medium containers. Wearing your dust mask and gloves, make a paste out of the dye powder and a small amount of very warm water. Once it is smooth, add the remaining warm water according to the following proportion: 1 tsp (5g) dye powder to $3/4$ cups (180mL) water, plus 1 fl. oz vinegar.

5. Set the containers of color aside to rest for at least 1 hour.

6. Move the containers to your work area and fill the Mason jars halfway with dyestock. Place the jars 1" (2.5cm) apart in the following order: #605 Pumpkin Orange, #604 Burnt Orange, #606 Deep Orange, #617 Cherry Red, #611 Vermillion.

7. Place a length of plastic wrap directly behind the dye jars. Give each jar a good stir.

dye the yarn

8. Remove your skein from the soak solution. Carefully squeeze out the excess water. Tidy the skein up if needed.

9. Fold the skein in half by matching the two figure 8s that determined the two ends of the skein (they should be different colors from the other figure 8s). Once folded in half, remove the larkshead knots (but not the figure 8s).

10. Place the end of the skein into the first dye jar, allow a portion of the skein to fall between the jars, and then place a portion of the skein into the next jar. Continue in this manner until the end of the skein goes into the last jar.

11. Allow this to sit for up to 15 minutes. What you want to see happening is for the color to creep up from the jar and into the skein. You do not want all the yellow between colors to be covered, so remove the skein before this happens.

STEP 6

STEP 10

STEP 11

STEP 12

STEP 12 (CONTINUED)

STEP 13

12. Carefully remove the skein from the first jar and lay it on the plastic wrap. Continue in this manner until the skein is fully stretched out on the plastic wrap. Wipe up any excess dye. Place another piece of plastic wrap on top and seal well.

13. Roll the packet into a coil, and allow the yarn to rest for at least 15 minutes before steaming. I find that this allows for better color saturation.

steam the yarn

14. Place water and a vegetable steamer in the pot. (The water should not touch the bottom of the vegetable steamer.) Place the coiled-up skein on top of the vegetable steamer. (I like to remove the lit-

tle post on the steamer; simply unscrew it to remove it.)

15. Steam for 30 minutes, starting the timer only once the water begins to boil. Take care that the water in the pot does not evaporate—add more water if necessary.

16. Turn off the heat and allow the packet to cool. This is very important. You will get better color and better adherence of the dyestuff if you let it cool thoroughly. Once your packet has cooled you can remove the plastic wrap. Never attempt to open a hot, plastic wrapped packet of yarn; the steam can burn you!

remove the yarn

17. Unwrap the cooled yarn and soak it in warm water and ¼ tsp (1.25mL) Synthrapol for about 5 minutes. Gently rinse the yarn 3–4 times in warm water. Do not agitate the yarn. Allow the yarn to air dry.

18. Once the yarn is dry, stretch the skeins back out under tension and wind into a ball.

Note You may have dyestock remaining; this can be kept stored in a sealed container for at least six months. You may need to warm up the stored dyestock before using.

half mitts

DESIGNED BY LINDA LA BELLE

I originally designed this Half Mitt for Gerald, our UPS man. Each Christmas I knit him a gift. A couple of years ago, having run out of ideas, I asked Gerald what he would like. He told me he wanted something that would keep his hands warm but his fingers free, and large enough to fit over his gloves. Here is a scaled-down version of Gerald's Half Mitts.

instructions

Cast on 40 stitches; divide on three needles (14, 12, 14). Join and place marker.

Work in k1, p1 ribbing in the round for 4½" (11.5cm) from cast-on edge. (The entire mitten is worked in k1, p1 ribbing.)

gusset

Work 20 stitches in pattern, then place marker. Bar increase in the next knit stitch, then immediately M1 in the next ladder. Place a marker, and work to end in ribbing as established (3 sts between markers).

Work 2 rounds in pattern, knitting stitches as they appear.

Next Rnd Work to marker; slip marker. Bar increase in the next knit stitch, then immediately M1 in the next ladder. P1, k1, slip the marker. Work to end (5 sts between markers).

Work 2 rnds in pattern.

Next Rnd Work to marker; slip marker. Bar increase in the next knit stitch, then immediately M1 in the next ladder. P1, k1, p1, k1, slip marker. Work to end (7 sts between markers).

Work 2 rnds in pattern.

Next Rnd Work to marker; slip marker. Bar increase in the next knit stitch, then immediately M1 in the next ladder. P1, k1, p1, k1, p1, k1; slip marker. Work to end (9 sts between markers).

Work 2 rnds in pattern.

Next Rnd Work to marker; pass marker. Do a bar increase in the next knit stitch, and immediately M1 in next ladder. P1, k1, p1, k1, p1, k1, p1, k1; pass marker. Work to end (11 sts between markers).

Work 2 rnds in pattern.

Next Rnd Work to marker; pass marker. Do a bar increase in the next knit stitch,

SKILL LEVEL
Intermediate

MATERIALS
- 2 balls Frog Tree 100% Alpaca Chunky, 1¾ oz (50g), 54 yds (49m)
- 1 set US #5 (3.75mm) double-pointed needles
- locking stitch markers
- tapestry needle

GAUGE
- In stockinette stitch
- 23 stitches and 29 rows = 4" (10cm)

SIZE
One size; approximately 9" (23cm) long

Abbreviations & Techniques

bar increase This is the perfect increase for this project. Once completed, it looks like a knit stitch and a purl stitch, so it continues the ribbing pattern.

Knit into the stitch from the front as usual; do not slip the stitch off the left-hand needle. Instead, bring the right-hand needle to the back of the loop on the left-hand needle. Slip the right-hand needle into the back of that loop, and knit it. Now you can slip the stitch from the left-hand needle. In essence, you are knitting into the front and then into the back of the same stitch.

(continued on page 83)

and immediately M1 in next ladder. P1, k1, p1, k1, p1, k1, p1, k1, p1, k1; pass marker. Work to end (13 sts between markers; 52 sts total).

Work 2 rnds in pattern.

Next Rnd Work to first marker; remove the marker, k1. Begin bind-off with the next purl stitch. Bind off 12 sts. (You will need to remove the second marker and use the first purl stitch after the marker in the bind-off.) Work to end (40 sts).

Next Rnd Work 21 sts in pattern; turn, and cast on 1 st. Turn, leaving the yarn in front. Pass the cast-on stitch from the right needle to the left needle. Purl the first 2 sts on the left needle together to join the work. Work to end (40 sts).

Work in pattern until the piece measures 8½" (21.5cm), or desired length, from the beginning.

finishing

Bind off in pattern.

Make the second half mitt identical to the first.

(continued from page 81)

M1 (make 1) Place the point of the left hand needle under the ladder between the first stitch on each needle from the back to the front, and place the ladder on the left hand needle. This will create a twisted stitch, and that is what you want. Knit the stitch. It takes a little patience to knit this stitch; the twisting makes it very tight and difficult to get the needle into. But it is well worth the effort, as it is an invisible increase.

SIMPLE YARN SUBSTITUTION

If you would like to make the Half Mitt but don't want to go to the trouble of dyeing the yarn, Frog Tree has the following yarn that will knit up in the same gauge: Frog Tree Chunky Alpaca Multitones, 100% Alpaca, 3½ oz (100g), 108 yds (99m).

jacquard handpainted silk

MATERIALS

- 1 oz Tiara 100% Silk Boucle from Henry's Attic, 2 oz (56g), 185 yds (169m)
- Jacquard Acid Dye, #639 Jet Black
- Synthrapol
- Distilled white vinegar
- Jacquard Super Clear

TOOLS

- Dust mask
- Gloves
- Enamel or stainless steel pot
- Measuring spoons
- Measuring cups
- Small whisks
- Plastic wrap
- 4 1" (2.5cm) sponge brushes
- 1 medium container in which to mix dyestock
- 4 small containers in which to mix your thickened colors
- Vegetable steamer

This yarn, which I named City Streets, and the handpainted yarn in Chapter 7, Springtime Boucle (page 128), are related projects. City Streets shows you what happens when you paint along the length of the skein, and Springtime Boucle shows you what happens when you paint across the width of the skein. For both projects, we will work with the same yarn but employ the two different techniques and two different dyes.

City Streets is a tone-on-tone project. To make this, we'll mix one dyestock and go from there.

prepare the yarn

1. Make the yarn into a 60" (152.5m) skein (page 16).

2. Soak the skein of silk in a dishpan with ½ tsp (2.5mL) Synthrapol, ¼ cup (60mL) vinegar, and warm water to cover.

prepare the dyestock

3. Put on your dust mask and gloves. In the medium container, make a paste of the dye with a small amount of very warm water.

4. Add the remaining warm water to equal the following proportion: 1 tbsp (15mL) Jet Black to ¾ cups (180mL) water. Set this container of dyestock aside to rest for at least 1 hour.

5. In small containers labeled with the color's intensity, mix up four shades of black as follows:

LIGHT: 1 tsp (5mL) stock + 1 tbsp (15mL) vinegar + 1 tbsp (15mL) Superclear. Add water to make ½ cup (120mL).

MEDIUM: 1 tbsp (15mL) stock + 1 tbsp (15mL) vinegar + 1 tbsp (15mL) Superclear. Add water to make ½ cup (120mL).

DARK: 5 tsp stock (25mL) + 1 tbsp (15mL) vinegar + 1 tbsp (15mL) Superclear. Add water to make ½ cup (120mL).

FULL: 1 tbsp (15mL) vinegar + 1 tbsp (15mL) Superclear. Add full-strength stock to make to make ½ cup (120mL).

paint the yarn

6. Remove the skein from the soak bath and squeeze out excess water. Place the skein on the plastic wrap, making the skein into an oval. If you can't fit the entire skein on your table, be sure to cover it, or place it in a large ziplock bag to prevent it from drying out!

7. Starting with your lightest color, paint along the skein as in the pictures. Do the same with the medium color, making the brush strokes a little shorter. Next comes the dark; your brush strokes should be shorter still. Finally, paint with the full-strength black. These strokes should be the shortest yet—be sure to leave white space!

8. Wipe up any excess dye that might have gotten on the plastic wrap, cover the yarn with another piece of plastic wrap, and seal. Allow the yarn to rest for at least 15 minutes before steaming. I find that this allows for better color saturation.

steam the yarn

9. Place water and a vegetable steamer in the pot. (The water should not touch the bottom of the vegetable steamer.) Place the coiled-up skein on top of the vegetable steamer. (I like to remove the little post; simply unscrew it to remove it.)

10. Steam for 30 minutes, starting the timer only once the water begins to boil. Take care that the water in the pot doesn't evaporate—add more water if necessary.

11. When the time is up, turn off the heat and allow the packet to cool completely in the pot. This is very important. You will get better color and better adherence of the dyestuff.

12. Remove the plastic wrap. Never attempt to open a hot, plastic-wrapped packet of yarn; the steam could burn you!

13. Rinse the yarn thoroughly in warm water. Allow to air dry.

14. Once the yarn is dry, stretch the skein back out under tension and wind into a ball.

STEP 7

STEP 7A

STEP 7B

STEP 7C

STEP 7D

STEP 7E

city streets scarf

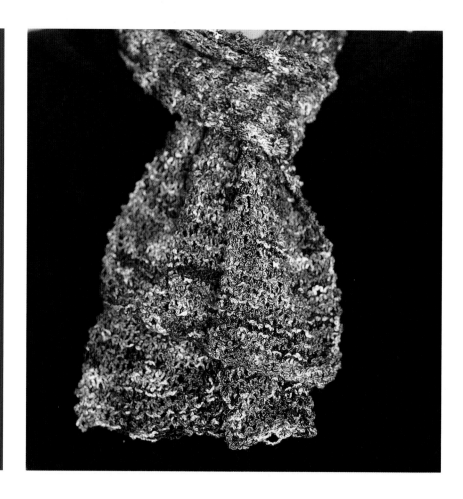

SIMPLE YARN SUBSTITUTION

If you would like to make this scarf but do not want to go to the trouble of dyeing your yarn, HABU Textiles has a beautiful silk boucle, #A-5 1/5 Kusaki Zome, naturally dyed, 100% silk, 1¹/₂ oz (42g), 233 yds (213m), which will knit up in a similar texture, using size US #8 (5mm) needles and 22 stitches. The sample swatch was knit up in color #36.

DESIGNED BY LINDA LA BELLE

This is a quick and easy scarf that looks great with jeans—or it can be dressy!

I recommend that you cast on and bind off with a needle at least two sizes larger than the needle you use for the main body, to keep the ends from being too tight.

instructions

Using larger needles, cast on 30 stitches. Switch to smaller needles and knit every row until you have 36" (91.5cm) of yarn left.

Bind off using larger needle.

jacquard handpainted alpaca

MATERIALS

- **6 skeins Catalina 100% Baby Alpaca Chunky, 3¹/₂ oz (100g), 109 yds (99m), color #101**
- **4 tbsp (60mL) gum tragacanth**
- **Jacquard Acid Dye, #639 Jet Black**
- **Citric acid**
- **Synthrapol**

TOOLS

- **Blender**
- **Measuring cups**
- **Measuring spoons**
- **Spatula**
- **Jar with lid that holds at least 1 qt (1L)**
- **Dust mask**
- **Gloves**
- **Enamel or stainless steel pot**
- **Small whisks**
- **Plastic wrap**
- **3 1" (2.5cm) sponge brushes**
- **1 2" (5cm) sponge brush**
- **1 medium container in which to mix dyestock**
- **4 small containers in which to mix your thickened colors**
- **Vegetable steamer**

A few years ago, Jen Fong, a woman who took classes at The Yarn Tree who happens to be a professional photographer, went on a trip to Iceland. On her return, she gave me a gift of a beautiful photo she had taken of an Icelandic sheep. When I went to Iceland myself a year later, I discovered firsthand just how difficult those sheep are to photograph! I fell in love with the way the Icelandic sweaters are constructed and thought that the same principles could be applied to a poncho. The tone-on-tone colors and the technique were definitely inspired by Jen's wonderful photo, which hangs in my studio.

The knitted project combines an already dyed yarn with the yarn you will dye yourself. I find that working with longer, skinnier skeins gives me the look that I want when handpainting yarn.

Icelandic sheep are allowed to roam free from spring until the fall, when they are rounded up. They are very independent and rather shy creatures.

prepare the gum tragacanth

Note You will mix the gum tragacanth in four separate mixtures. Each time you finish one, transfer it to the jar using the spatula to ensure that you remove all the prepared gum tragacanth from the blender before you mix up the next batch. You can store the gum tragacanth preparation covered in the refrigerator for several months.

1. Place 1 cup (250mL) of boiling water in the blender. With the blender on high speed, slowly sprinkle 1 tbsp (15g) gum tragacanth, and allow the mixture to blend completely. Transfer to a jar.

2. Repeat 3 more times.

STEP 8

STEP 11

STEP 11 (CONTINUED)

prepare the yarn

3. Wind each of the six skeins into balls and then make those balls back into skeins that are 12 yds (11m) long.

4. Soak all the yarn in a dishpan with 4 tsp (20mL) Synthrapol, 12 tbsp (180mL) citric acid, and 2 gal (8L) warm water. Allow the yarn to soak for 1 hour.

prepare the dyestock

4. Put on your dust mask and gloves. In the medium container, make a paste of the dye powder with a small amount of very warm water. Once it is smooth, add the remaining warm water according to the following proportion: 1 tbsp (15mL) Jet Black to 3/4 cups (180mL) water.

5. Set the stock aside to rest for at least 1 hour.

6. In separate small containers, mix up different shades of dye:

LIGHT: 1 tbsp (15mL) dyestock + 1 tbsp (15mL) water + 2 tbsp (30mL) prepared gum tragacanth.

MEDIUM: 3 tbsp (45mL) dyestock + 1 tbsp (15mL) water + 2 tbsp (30mL) prepared gum tragacanth.

DARK: 5 tbsp (75mL) dyestock + 1 tbsp water (15mL) + 2 tbsp (30mL) prepared gum tragacanth.

FULL: 12 tbsp (180mL) dyestock + 2 tbsp (30mL) prepared gum tragacanth.

paint the yarn

7. Remove the skeins from the soak bath and squeeze out excess water.

8. Place all six skeins on the plastic wrap. Lay the first one out on the work surface, snaking it back and forth. Butt up the ends, continuing to snake along the work surface. Do this until you have laid out all six skeins.

9. For this painting technique, you will make your brush strokes different lengths and different shapes. Be sure to leave white space between your brush strokes. (I am calling them brush strokes, but you are really dabbing on the surface of the yarn.)

10. Using a tape measure, mark out approximately 12- to 14-inch (30cm) sections. If your work surface can't accommodate this, set it up so your repeat divides as evenly as possible into the length of the area to be painted.

11. Starting with your lightest color, paint across the width of the skeins in a line the width of the brush as in the picture. Do the same with the medium color, making short brush strokes on an angle. Next comes the dark; your brush strokes should be across the width of the skein using only the tip of the brush to make a very narrow line. Finally, paint with the full-strength black. These strokes will be long and wide.

12. Repeat this pattern along the length of your skein until the whole skein is painted.

13. Place plastic wrap over the entire area of painted yarn. There is too much yarn to turn the skein over; instead, take a piece of PVC pipe or an old rolling pin, and roll over the surface of the skeins to force the color to the underside of the

STEP 11 (CONTINUED)

STEP 11 (CONTINUED)

STEP 13

skeins. Roll from both directions several times. The viscosity of the gum tragacanth makes this work.

14. Seal up the plastic wrap and allow the yarn to rest for at least 15 minutes before steaming. I find that this allows for better color saturation.

steam the yarn

15. Place water and a vegetable steamer in the pot. (The water should not touch the bottom of the vegetable steamer.)

Place the coiled up skein on top of the vegetable steamer. (I like to remove the little post; simply unscrew it to remove it.) Steam for 45 minutes, starting the timer only once the water begins to boil. Do not to let the water evaporate—add more water if necessary.

16. Turn off the heat and allow the yarn to cool completely in the pot (this may take several hours). This is very important. You will get better color and better adherence of the dyestuff.

remove the yarn

17. Remove the plastic wrap. Never attempt to open a hot, plastic-wrapped packet of yarn; the steam could burn you!

18. Soak the yarn in warm water with ¼ tsp (1.25mL) Synthrapol for about 5 minutes. Gently rinse the yarn 3-4 times in warm water. Do not agitate the yarn. Allow your yarn to air dry.

19. Once the yarn is dry, stretch the skeins back out under tension and wind into a ball.

hooded poncho

Technique

three-needle bind-off Place half of the stitches on another needle. Holding the right (knit) sides together, insert a third needle that is two sizes larger than the working needle into the first stitch on each left-hand needle at the same time. Knit these two stitches as if they are one. You will have one stitch on the right hand needle. Repeat. Now you will have two stitches on the right-hand needle. Pass the right stitch over the left stitch and off the needle. Continue in this manner until you have one stitch remaining on your right needle. Cut a long tail, and pass the tail through the last stitch.

DESIGNED BY LINDA LA BELLE

I n the fall of 2002, while on my way to France for the Paris premiere of Matthew Barney's final film in the Cremaster Cycle, *Cremaster 3*, on which I worked as the costume designer, I made a side trip to Iceland. While visiting the shops in Reykjavik, I was able to take a close look at the construction of the traditional Icelandic sweater. I immediately fell in love with the simplicity of the design and thought it would translate well to a poncho. I knew that baby alpaca would give wonderful drape to the knitted fabric. Here is the result—I hope you like it!

instructions

With MC, cast on 221 stitches. Turn. Being careful not to twist, slip the last cast-on stitch from the right-hand needle onto the left-hand needle, so it sits next to the slip knot. Place a marker on the right needle to mark the beginning of the round. Knit the first two stitches on the left needle together (220 sts). Pull the yarn firmly to prevent a gap. (On each round, when you come to the marker, slip it to the right needle and keep knitting.) This will be the first knit stitch of your rib pattern.

Work ribbing in MC yarn as follows:

K3, p5 around for 3" (7.5cm) from cast-on edge.

Begin stockinette (in the round you only need to knit to achieve stockinette stitch).

Work 2 rounds still using the MC yarn.

Switch to CC and work 2 rounds.

At the marker, switch to MC, being sure to pick up MC from underneath CC. Work 2 rounds.

At the marker, switch to CC, being sure to pick up CC from underneath MC. Work 2 rounds.

Note Be sure to twist your yarns when changing colors by picking up the new color from below the old color.

Repeat these 4 rounds until you have a total of 12" (30.5cm) from the cast-on edge.

decrease

Note To make it less confusing, your original marker should be a different color than the markers you are about to place on the needle.

Keeping in your stripe pattern, knit 20 stitches and place marker. Repeat this nine more times, end knit 20. You are back at your original marker.

Rnd 1 Knit until 2 stitches before first marker; k2tog. Repeat around the needle, knitting 2 stitches together before each marker (209 sts).

Rnds 2–4 Knit.

Repeat these 4 rounds until there are 77 sts remaining.

Next Rnd K2tog, knit to end, removing all markers except original marker (76 sts). End with 2 rounds in MC. This may require knitting 2 more rounds. This makes for a smoother transition.

neck

With MC, work in k2, p2 ribbing on all stitches for 2½" (6.5cm).

hood

You will now be working back and forth with right side facing and starting at the marker. You will also have three bobbins of yarn—2 bobbins of MC and 1 bobbin of CC.

Row 1 With first MC bobbin, k2, bind off the next 2 purl stitches. Work the next seven stitches in seed stitch as follows: k1, p1, k1, p1, k1, p1, k1. With CC, knit to the last seven stitches. With second MC bobbin, repeat seed stitch as follows: k1, p1, k1, p1, k1, p1, k1.

Row 2 With MC bobbin, work the first seven stitches in seed stitch as follows: k1, p1, k1, p1, k1, p1, k1. Switch to the CC bobbin, being sure to pick up CC from underneath MC. With CC, purl to the last seven stitches. Switch to the MC bobbin, being sure to pick up MC from underneath CC. With MC, repeat seed stitch as follows: k1, p1, k1, p1, k1, p1, k1.

Repeat these 2 rows for a total of 12" (30.5cm), ending with a right side row.

Finish the hood with a three-needle bind-off and MC. Weave in the tail.

THIS PAGE, CLOCKWISE FROM TOP LEFT: Mary Paddon immersion dyes an 8/2 reeled silk yarn. Mary's dogs, Coal and Smiley, on their best behavior, greet people at the door. Cheryl Huseby Wiebe prepares to dye in her studio. Silk ribbon for the Montano Series (colorway Twig), dyed by Cheryl, is ready to be wrapped up and sent to the steamer. Mary sprinkles dye on wool roving to produce a variegated dyed roving in the Blue Symphony colorway. OPPOSITE PAGE, LEFT TO RIGHT: Karen Selk's dog, Annie, on the porch ready to greet visitors to Treenway Silks. Step inside the doors of Treenway Silks and you will find an abundance of hand-dyed silk yarns, ribbons, and rovings displayed in more than 100 colors.

KAREN SELK OF TREENWAY SILKS

WITH MARY PADDON AND
CHERYL HUSEBY WIEBE

Treenway Silks is located on the south side of Salt Spring Island in British Columbia, Canada. To get there, I flew to Victoria on Vancouver Island, rented a car, and then took a ferry to Salt Spring Island.

Owned by Karen Selk and her husband, Terry Nelson, Treenway specializes in silk. Thirty yarns, five ribbons, fibers, cocoons, hankies, caps, silk waste, silk blends—the shelves at Treenway are overflowing with beautiful silk products. All of the silk can be purchased undyed or dyed to order in one hundred colors! They also produce a line of hand-dyed wool roving, favored by many a spinner.

Treenway started out thirty years ago, in the late '70s, selling only the undyed yarns. Then they began dyeing to order, contracting the dyeing out. This is how the business is still run today, now employing six dyers. The business was moved from Victoria, British Columbia, to Salt Spring in 2001.

The majority of the silks are imported from China and the balance from India. It is important to Karen to

visit the villages where the yarns are produced. To this end, she travels to China every two to four years. Karen and Terry are planning a visit to India soon.

Karen had arranged for me to interview two of her dyers, Cheryl Huseby Wiebe and Mary Paddon. Both live on the north side of Salt Spring Island. Cheryl and Mary are precision dyers (the art of paying attention to how much dye and fiber you are putting together), and they dye everything that Treenway has to offer. This means that in one day they could be dyeing wool roving, silk top, silk ribbon, and silk yarn. It could be immersion dyeing, sprinkle dyeing, or variegated dyeing.

While I was there I got to see Mary immersion dyeing 8/2 silk and silk ribbon and also sprinkle dyeing Corriedale Roving in "Blue Symphony." I saw Cheryl handpaint Tussah silk roving (Salt Spring series) and silk ribbon in "Twig" (Montano series). I was really in for a treat!

I had heard that the water on Salt Spring Island was perfect for dyeing silk, so I asked Karen, Mary, and Cheryl about it. It turns out that depending

where you live on the island, the water can vary—another dyer lives by Mount Maxwell, and her water is very soft, while both Cheryl and Mary's water is very hard. (Mary finds that she uses more acid in her dyebath than most dye recipes would call for.) So, in the end it is not the water on Salt Spring, but the dyers who are perfect!

I went to Mary's on my second day on the island, and as I pulled into the driveway I was greeted with great excitement by Coal and Smiley, Mary's Labrador retrievers. Mary's dye studio, Deer Haven, sits under the shade of trees, and it is aptly named: A doe and her offspring stopped by for apples while I was there! The studio is a long narrow space, where Mary likes to work in quiet. What a lovely quiet it is—I could hear the birds, the wind rustling the leaves, and every now and again Smiley and Coal would remind me that they were around, too. Plus, the ocean is just a short walk away.

Cheryl's home is up a hill, under the shade of trees with a view of the water. She and her husband, John, run a small-scale farm with sheep, llamas, and chickens, visiting ducks, and pet cats.

They also have a garden, and they sell their eggs and produce at an honor system roadside stand. As Cheryl was showing me around her dye studio, there was a noise at the door. It was Fergus, a very friendly Shetland sheep, wanting to come in and see what was going on. Later, we went outside so that I could get a look at the animals, and suddenly a llama was sniffing me! Suntos, the extremely curious llama, had his nose in my face sniffing up a storm. It turns out that this is the llama way of getting to know you.

It is hard to tell either Mary or Cheryl's story without including the other—they are best friends. Though they have very different personalities, they can both reproduce the same techniques on yarns and fibers—it's no easy feat to have that kind of discipline and self-control. One has to be able to set her ego aside and understand that it is the end product that is important. Mary is a spinner and weaver, Cheryl a spinner. They have been working for Karen for six years, ever since Treenway moved from Victoria to Salt

Spring Island. Cheryl and Mary met through a now-defunct fiber co-op, and they met Karen at workshops that Karen had given several years earlier.

The ribbons, yarns, and fibers are a collaboration between Karen and her dyers. Karen is not a dyer herself—she's a weaver—but she has a great color sense. The dyers are constantly exploring how the colors can be applied to the various substrates. Both Cheryl and Mary are welcome to give suggestions and comments.

When Karen decided to collaborate with Judith Montano for the Montano series (variegated silk ribbon and silk cord), it took Mary and Cheryl two years of testing to work out the seventy-five colorways, and it took months to work out the kinks in the Salt Spring series, variegated dyeing on Tussah silk roving.

Patience is a key word in their vocabulary. Detailed note-taking and communication with each other is also very important. Cheryl's secret to dyeing is that precision dyeing is not all that difficult! Mary says her inspiration is all

around her. She told me of rounding the corner of her deck one evening as the sun was setting. The gold of the sun, green of the foliage, and blues of the sky and water would become "Blue Symphony."

I asked Cheryl what advice she would give to someone starting out. "Learn the basics: Understand your dyes. If you're precision dyeing, invest in a good set of measuring devices, a scale, and a thermometer; organize your workspace so that it is convenient and efficient; pay attention to the safety issues; and beware of repetitive movements that can wear on your body."

These days, Karen and Terry are building a new home on their land. They will move out of the converted barn and into a real house that will be situated on a hill above their garden and facing the ocean.

My time on Salt Spring passed all too quickly. Suddenly it was Saturday morning and time to head out for the ferry, my head filled with the beauty of the island and its people!

THIS PAGE, CLOCKWISE FROM TOP LEFT: Stainless steel dyepots sit outside Cheryl's studio, supported on a rack made by her husband, John. Raw silk yarn and silk cocoons on display at Treenway Silks. These silk yarns represent just a few of the one hundred hand-dyed colors available from Treenway Silks. Fergus, the curious sheep, comes into the studio to see what's going on. Artichokes in Karen's garden, which we ate that evening. OPPOSITE PAGE, LEFT TO RIGHT: Karen passes the shuttle through the warp shed. Karen Selk works at her loom in her sunlit studio.

6

procion mx fiber reactive dyes

The dye used in this chapter is different from all the other dyes I have chosen for the book.

Procion MX dyes are fiber reactive dyes. This means that the color is developed inside the fiber, not on the surface of the fiber. This gives a permanent color that is both light-fast and wash-fast. The dye was developed for use on cellulosic fibers such as cotton, linen, and ramie, and it can also be used on protein fibers such as wool, silk, and nylon. In order for the dyes to work with cellulosic fibers, the solution must be alkaline (adding sodium carbonate), while with protein fibers the solution must be acidic (using acetic acid for the sodium carbonate). The alkaline-based dyestuff sets up after sitting wrapped in plastic for 24 to 48 hours, but acidic bases require heat to set the color.

For our dye projects in this chapter, we will be working with two different cottons using a handpainting technique and then allowing our skeins to sit wrapped in plastic for 48 hours.

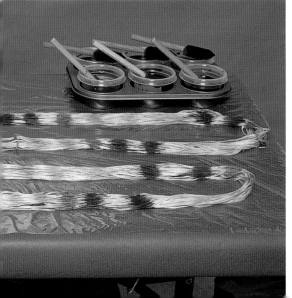

procion mx handpainted cotton

MATERIALS

- **A-173-000 Kasuri Cotton from HABU Textiles, 100% cotton, 2 oz (56g), 130 yds (129m)**
- **Synthrapol**
- **Soda ash**
- **Pro Print Paste SH**
- **Urea**
- **Metaphos (if you have hard water)**
- **Baking soda**
- **Procion MX Fiber Reactive Dye in the following colors: #184 Bubblegum, #042 Raspberry**

TOOLS

- **Measuring cups and spoons**
- **12-inch (30cm) ruler**
- **4 containers for prepared dye**
- **1 wide-mouth jar, 2-cup (500mL), for the print paste**
- **1 wide-mouth jar, 1 qt (1L), for the urea**
- **1 small container with a lid for alkali powder**

I asked Yvette Byas what color she would like for the flowers to go on the Crochet Shawl (page 72). With a smile, she pointed to a vase on the table. It was filled with light pink peonies and white roses that were tipped in a very deep pink.

The flowers had been a gift from a woman who had taken spinning classes at the shop, and the colors were a perfect contrast for the green of the Crochet Shawl.

prepare the yarn

1. Begin by making the cotton yarn into a skein that is 30 ft (9m) in length. In a dishpan, to 1 qt (1L) hot water add 1/4 tsp (1.25mL) Synthrapol, 1 tsp (5g) soda ash, and your skein. Leave this to soak for 1 hour.

prepare the print paste

2. Pour 1 cup (250mL) warm 110°F (44°C) water into the wide-mouth jar. Sprinkle 5 1/2 tbsp (55g) print paste powder into

STEP 8

STEP 9

STEP 9 (CONTINUED)

the water while stirring rapidly. Stir until you have a smooth paste. Let stand for 1 hour (or overnight). The prepared print paste (without dye added) can be stored for up to six months, normally without refrigeration, in an airtight container.

prepare the urea

3. Mix up the urea water as follows: 3 tbsp (45mL) urea with 1 qt (1L) warm 110°F (44°C) water. (If you have hard water, add 1 tsp [5mL] Metaphos.) Allow to cool before using. (The urea water can be stored at room temperature in a closed container. If you detect an ammonia smell, you must discard it.)

prepare the mixed alkali powder

4. In a medium wide-mouth jar, place 4 tbsp (43g) baking soda and 1 tbsp (9g) soda ash, mix well. The mixed alkali powder can be stored for up to six months in an airtight container. After that, it should be discarded.

prepare the dyestock

5. Mark your four medium containers as follows: raspberry light, raspberry medium, raspberry dark, and bubblegum.

6. Put on your gloves and dust mask. Place 1/8 tsp (0.5g) Raspberry dye powder in the light container; 1/2 tsp (2g) in the medium container; 1 tsp (5g) in the dark container; and 1/8 tsp (0.5g) Bubblegum dye powder in the bubblegum container. Make a paste of each dye powder using a small amount of urea water, then add the following to each container: 1 tsp (5g) prepared print paste, 1/4 tsp (1g) mixed alkali powder, and urea water to make 1/4 cup (60mL).

paint the yarn

7. Remove the skein from the soak solution and gently squeeze out the excess water. When you place the skein on plastic wrap, snake it on the table.

8. Place the ruler along the skein and paint with the bubblegum first, using the flat of the brush. Dab the color 12" (30cm) apart, working around the length of the skein.

9. Using the tip of a clean brush for each color, fill in the skein, first with the light raspberry, then the medium raspberry, and finally the dark raspberry, being

sure to leave white space between each color. Once you are done painting, allow the yarn to sit uncovered for 15 minutes. I find that allowing the yarn to sit before wrapping up in the plastic wrap allows better color penetration. While the yarn is resting, be sure to mop up any pools of color that may have accumulated.

10. Wrap the skein in plastic wrap; you may need two long pieces placed side by side with an overlap. Press down around the yarn to seal. Seal around the outside edges by folding the package in thirds. Do not roll—fold it flat.

11. Place this package in a black trash bag and leave in a warm spot for 48 hours.

rinse the yarn

12. Unwrap the yarn and place it in a basin of warm water, 75-95°F (24-35°C). Change the rinse water 3-4 times, then wash with very hot water 140°F (60°C), adding 1/4 tsp (1.25mL) Synthrapol. Rinse well and allow to dry.

13. Once dry place back under tension and wind into a ball.

STEP 10

STEP 10 (CONTINUED)

STEP 10 (CONTINUED)

crochet flowers

DESIGNED BY YVETTE BYAS AND LINDA LA BELLE

These flowers are designed to go on the crocheted shawl on page 72, but use them to adorn your lapel, a hat, or anything else your heart desires!

SKILL LEVEL
Beginner

MATERIALS
- A-173-000 Kasuri Cotton from HABU Textiles, 100% cotton, 1 oz (28.5g), 65 yds (59m)

- 1 US H-8 (5mm) crochet hook

- tapestry needle

SIZE
Approximately 1¹/₂" (3.8cm) across

Abbreviations

ch chain

sc single crochet

sl st slip stitch

hdc half double crochet

instructions

Ch 4, then join with a sl st in the first ch from hook to form a ring.

Rnd 1 Ch 1. Make 8 sc in the ring, join with a sl st in first sc to form a ring.

Rnd 2 Ch 2 (counts as 1 hdc). Work 2 hdc in the first sc, then 1 sl st in the next sc. (1 sl st, ch 2, 2 hdc) in the same stitch. Sl st in the next sc. (1 sl st, ch 2, 2 hdc) in the same stitch. Repeat all the way around until you have five petals.

Fasten off. Leave a long tail to sew flower onto shawl. Weave in any other ends.

Make 30 flowers.

attaching flowers to shawl

Space the flowers about 2" (5cm) from the finished edge and about 5" (12.5cm) apart, to fit 13 flowers on each side. Place two flowers about 3" (7.5cm) apart in the center of the other 2 flowers on each end.

SIMPLE YARN SUBSTITUTION

If you do not wish to dye the yarn, HABU has this same yarn dyed with natural dyes!

procion mx handpainted confetti cotton

MATERIALS

- **2 skeins Island Cotton IV from Henry's Attic, 98% pima cotton, 2% nylon, 8 oz (226g), 370 yds (338m)**

  Make 5 new skeins as follows:

  - **One 8-oz (226g) skein 10 yds (9m) in diameter for confetti skein**

  - **Four 2-oz skeins 2 yds (1.8m) in diameter for solid coordinating skeins (page 106)**

- **4 tbsp (60mL) gum tragacanth**

- **Procion MX Fiber Reactive Dye in the following colors: #030 Fire Engine Red, #094 Emerald Green, #079 Midnight Blue, #010 Bright Golden yellow**

- **Synthrapol**

- **Soda ash**

- **Baking soda**

TOOLS

- **Blender**
- **Measuring cups**
- **Measuring spoons**
- **Spatula**
- **Gloves**
- **Dust mask**
- **12" (30cm) ruler**
- **4 wide-mouth jars, 2 cup (500mL) for prepared dye**
- **1 wide-mouth jar, 1 qt (1L) for gum tragacanth**

For this yarn, I wanted to get variations of color within the color. To achieve this, I decided to thicken the dyestock with gum tragacanth, a natural thickening agent.

When I was planning out the dye pattern, I made a sketch using magic markers on paper and followed that sketch as a guide for my painting technique.

The test drive was when I put the sweater on Namiko, our model. Would she fuss, I wondered? Nope! She happily wore the sweater and hat for the three hours the photo shoot took!

prepare the gum tragacanth

Note You will mix the gum tragacanth in four separate mixtures. Each time you finish one, transfer it to the jar using the spatula to ensure that you remove all the prepared gum tragacanth from the blender before you mix up the next batch. You can store the gum tragacanth preparation covered in the refrigerator for several months.

1. Place 1 cup (250mL) of boiling water in the blender. With the blender on high speed, slowly sprinkle 1 tbsp (15mL) gum

STEP 7

STEP 8

tragacanth, and allow the mixture to blend completely. Transfer to the jar.

2. Repeat 3 more times.

prepare the yarn

3. To 4 qt (4L) hot water in a dishpan, add ½ tsp (1.25mL) Synthrapol, 2 tsp (5g) soda ash, and your skeins. Leave this to soak for 1 hour.

prepare the dye paste

4. Wearing gloves and dust mask, measure ½ tsp (2g) dye powder into each of 4 labeled wide-mouth jars, then make a paste with a small amount of warm water. Add 4 fl. oz (120mL) prepared gum tragacanth and mix well, then add 3 oz (90mL) warm (110°F [44°C]) water and mix well. Set aside for 1 hour.

paint the yarn

5. Add 1 tsp (5g) baking soda to each of the 4 jars of thickened color. From this point, you will only have about 2 hours to paint before the dye is no longer activated and you will not be able to use it.

6. Remove only the 8-oz (226g) skein from the soak solution, gently squeeze out any excess water, and place it on plastic wrap, making an open oval with the skein. If your work table is not long enough, place what doesn't fit inside a large ziplock bag or cover it so that the skein doesn't dry out when you work on the accessible sections.

7. Set a 12" (30cm) ruler next to the yarn, and, using the flat of the brush and the thickened red dye, paint across the skein at the 1" (2.5cm) mark, as shown. Repeat at the 11" (30cm) mark. Do this around the entire skein (or as far as you can go on the exposed yarn). A note about painting this skein: Don't feel that every brush stroke or the white space you leave has to be the same length or width. It is the variation that gives this yarn life. You will not be turning this skein over to paint the other side, so press a bit on the skein with the brush. Varying the pressure will give you more shades of color in the end result!

8. Paint with the thickened green dye. I only painted half the width of the skein with this color, and I left space between the red and the green. Distribute the color how you like.

9. It is now time for the third color, the thickened yellow dye. On the sample skein, I painted below the green, and again on the top half edge of the skein next to the red. Repeat this around.

10. Paint the thickened blue dye in the remaining space, being sure to not fill the entire space (i.e., leave some white space).

11. Place plastic wrap over it, seal the center so the skein doesn't touch itself, and seal the edges. Allow to sit for 15 minutes before folding up.

12. Place the folded skein in a black plastic garbage bag and leave in a warm spot for 48 hours.

rinse the yarn

13. Remove the skein from the plastic wrap and place the yarn in a basin of warm water, 75–95°F (24–35°C). Change the rinse water 3–4 times, then wash with very hot water, 140°F (60°C), adding ¼ tsp (1.25mL) Synthrapol. Rinse well and air dry.

14. Once the yarn is dry, stretch the skein back out under tension and wind into a ball.

STEP 9

STEP 10

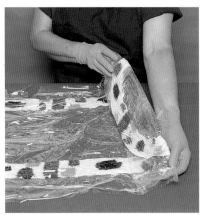

STEP 11

STEP 1

STEP 2

STEP 2

procion mx handpainted solid cotton

MATERIALS
See page 104

You should have enough dyestock remaining from painting the multicolored skein (page 104) to make coordinating solid skeins. If not, please follow the directions on page 104 to mix up your dyestuff.

You might have noticed that these are not really solid colors in the sense that the color is distributed evenly throughout. Instead, through the use of gum traga-canth, we will get a lovely subtle variation of color on each of the solid skeins.

paint the yarn

1. Remove one of the smaller skeins from the soak solution and gently squeeze out the excess water. Place on plastic wrap. Using a 2" (5cm) sponge brush and one of the coordinating colors, paint the skein by pressing down with the sponge brush and dragging it across the surface of the yarn. Vary the pressure; this will help to variegate the skein.

2. Once the top is fully painted, flip the skein over and paint the other side in the same manner.

3. Check inside the skein to be sure no white areas are showing. Wrap the skein in plastic wrap and seal the edges. Place the skein in a black plastic garbage bag and leave in a warm spot for 48 hours. Repeat with the three remaining skeins, each wrapped separately and placed in the garbage bag.

rinse the yarn

4. Remove the skeins from the plastic wrap and rinse each separately as follows: Place the yarn in a basin of warm water, 75–95°F (24-35°C). Change the rinse water 3–4 times, then wash with very hot water, 140°F (60°C), adding ¼ tsp (1.25mL) Synthrapol. Rinse well and air dry.

5. Once the yarn is dry, stretch the skein back out under tension and wind into a ball.

confetti sweater

Abbreviations & Techniques

k2tog Knit 2 stitches together.

knit pick up Insert the tip of the right-hand needle under the edge stitch, wrap the yarn, and pull the loop through.

DESIGNED BY LINDA LA BELLE

I made this sweater with a little girl in mind. If you are making it for a boy, simply put the buttonholes on the left band and the buttons on the right.

instructions

back

With Color A, cast on 44 (48, 52) sts with the US #8 (5mm) needle. Change to the US #5 (3.75mm) needles and work in k1, p1 ribbing for 1" (2.5cm).

Change to the US #6 (4mm) needle and MC, and knit in stockinette stitch until piece measures 6 (6½, 7¼)" (15 [16.5, 18.5]cm) from the cast-on edge. At the same time, increase 1 st on each side at rows 9, 19, 29, and 39 for a total of 52 (56, 60) sts.

Hint On every purl row, knit the first and last stitch. This will make the sweater much easier to sew up!

armhole

Bind off 6 sts at the beginning of the next 2 rows (40 (44, 48) sts). Continue in stockinette stitch, until piece measures 10½ (11¼, 12¼)" (26.5 [28.5, 31]cm) from cast-on edge. End with a purl row. Distribute remaining stitches onto 3 stitch holders as follows: (11, 18, 11) ([13, 18, 13], [15, 18, 15]).

right front

Hint Work both fronts at the same time on one needle with two balls of yarn, being sure to reverse the shaping. This way you are guaranteed that they will knit up the same!

With Color A and the US #8 (5mm) needles, cast on 22 (24, 26) sts. Using the US #5 (3.75cm) needles, work in ribbing as for back.

Change to the US #6 (4mm) needles and MC. At the same time, increase 1 st at the beginning of rows 9, 19, 29, and 39 for a total of 26 (28, 30) sts. Knit in stockinette stitch until piece measures 6 (6½, 7¼)" (15 [16.5, 18.5]cm) from the cast-on edge. End with a knit row.

Bind off 6 sts at the beginning of the next row for armhole (20 [22, 24] sts).

Continue in stockinette stitch until piece measures 8½ (9¼, 9¾)" (21.5 [23.5, 24.8]cm) from the beginning. End with a knit row.

one row buttonhole This technique makes a strong horizontal buttonhole over 5 stitches, by binding off in one direction and casting on in the other. Work to the first buttonhole stitch, and bring your yarn to the front. Slip one stitch purlwise (without twisting), then bring your yarn to the back. *Slip the next stitch (again without twisting). Pass the first slipped stitch over the second slipped stitch and off of the needle*. Repeat from * to * 3 more times.

Now that you have bound off 4 stitches, turn your work. With the yarn in back, cast on 5 stitches using the cable cast-on method.

Insert the right-hand needle between the first and second stitches on the left-hand needle, wrap your yarn, and draw the loop through. Place this loop on the left-hand needle. Repeat from * to *.

Now turn your work back to the original side. With the yarn in back, slip the first stitch (without twisting), and pass the last cast-on stitch over it and off of the right-hand needle. Continue, working in pattern until you reach the next buttonhole.

right front neck drop

Purl to last 5 sts and place these 5 sts on holder. Turn, and bind off 2 sts. Knit to the end (13 [15, 17] sts).

Next Row Purl.

Bind off 1 st at center front every other row 2 times (11 [13, 15] sts).

Continue in stockinette stitch until piece measures 10½ (11¼, 12¼)" (26.5 [28.5, 31]cm) from cast-on edge. Place 11 (13, 15) sts on holder.

left front

Work as for Right Front, reversing all shaping, up to Right Front Neck Drop.

left front neck drop

Purl first 5 sts, place on a holder. Bind off 2 sts. Purl to the end of row (13 [15, 17] sts).

Next Row Knit.

Bind off 1 st at center front every other row 2 times (11 [13, 15] sts).

Continue in stockinette stitch until piece measures 10½ (11¼, 12¼)" (26.5 [28.5, 31]cm) from cast-on edge.

shoulder

Work a three-needle bind-off for right shoulder stitches as follows:

With right sides together, slip stitches of Right Front and Right Back shoulders to 2 double-pointed needles. With right side facing and needles parallel, insert third double-pointed needle into first stitch of each needle and knit these stitches together, slipping stitches off left-hand needles. *Knit next 2 stitches together in the same way. Slip first stitch on right-hand needle over second stitch and off needle.

Repeat from * until all stitches are bound off.

Repeat for left shoulder.

sleeves

With right side facing and using MC and the US #6 (4mm) needle, knit pick up 46 (50, 54) stitches along the armhole, starting at the right edge and ending at the left edge.

Row 1 Purl.

Row 2 Knit.

Row 3 Purl.

Row 4 Knit, and at the same time, decrease 1 stitch by knitting 2 stitches together at the beginning and end of the row.

Continue in this manner, decreasing every fourth row until 22 (26, 30) sts remain.

Continue in stockinette stitch until the sleeve measures 6¾ (7¼, 8)" (17 [18.5,

20.5]cm) from cast-on edge.

Change to the US #5 (3.75mm) needles and Color B, and work in k1, p1 ribbing for 1" (2.5cm).

Bind off in ribbing using the US #8 (5mm) needles.

Note It is important that the sleeve bind-off be loose. Small children tend to make a fist when putting on a sweater.

Repeat for second sleeve.

neck band

Note The double-pointed needle is used only to transfer stitches off the holder. You will then knit the stitches from the double-pointed needle onto the US #5 (3.75mm) single-point needle.

With right side facing, place 5 sts from holder onto dpn. Using Color C and smaller needle, knit those sts. Knit pick up 5 (7, 9) sts. Place 18 sts from holder onto dpn and knit. Knit pick up 5 (7, 9) sts. Place 5 sts from holder onto dpn and knit (38 [42, 46] sts).

Working back and forth, work 4 rows of k1, p1 ribbing. Bind off in ribbing using the US #8 (5mm) needle.

left front band

Note This is the side with the buttons.

With right side facing, using Color D and a US #5 (3.75mm) needle, knit pick up 54 (60, 64) sts along front edge.

Work 7 rows of k1, p1 ribbing.

Bind off in ribbing on the same needle.

right front band

Note This is the side with the buttonholes.

With right side facing, using Color D and the US #5 (3.75mm) needles, knit pick up 54 (60, 64) sts along front edge.

Work 3 rows of k1, p1 ribbing.

Next row Work 3 (3, 4) sts in pattern; work one-row buttonhole. *Work 9 (11, 12) sts in pattern, then work one-row buttonhole*; repeat from * to * 2 more times, ending with 4 sts in pattern.

Work 3 more rows of k1, p1 ribbing.

Bind off in ribbing on the same needle.

finishing

Sew sleeve and side seam as one long seam, using invisible weaving technique.

Invisible Weaving This technique makes an invisible seam for stockinette stitch projects. Place the pieces next to each other and right side up on a flat surface. Thread your tapestry needle.

Starting at the bottom of your seam, in the first full stitch in from the edge, *insert the needle under the ladder (horizontal bar). Next, insert the needle under the ladder on the other piece. Pull the yarn through, being careful to pull in the direction of the seam and not toward yourself*. Repeat from * to * until you have finished the seam. Weave in the ends.

SIMPLE YARN SUBSTITUTION

If you fell in love with the Confetti Sweater but you do not wish to dye the yarn, I found the perfect substitution yarn. It is Sandra from the Schaefer Yarn Co., 78% cotton, 22% rayon, 6 oz (171g), 225 yds (205m). We were able to keep the same needle size and match the gauge. The sample swatch for the Sandra yarn is knit up in "Martha Graham."

confetti hat with top knot

SKILL LEVEL
Intermediate

MATERIALS
- 4 oz (113g), 185 yds (169m), Alpine Cotton IV from Henry's Attic, 98% pima cotton, 2% nylon

2 oz (5 g) Main Color

1 oz (28g) each of 2 Contrast Colors (B and D)

- 1 16" (40.5cm) US #6 (4mm) circular needle

- 1 set US #6 (4mm) double-pointed needles

- stitch marker

- tapestry needle

GAUGE
- In stockinette stitch

- 18 stitches and 30 rows = 4" (10cm)

SIZE
0 to 6 months (6 months to 1 year, toddler)

Abbreviations

k2tog Knit 2 stitches together.

SIMPLE YARN SUBSTITUTION

If you fell in love with the Confetti Hat but you do not wish to dye the yarn, I found the perfect substitution yarn. It is Sandra from the Schaefer Yarn Co., 78% cotton, 22% rayon, 6 oz (171g), 225 yds (205m). We were able to keep the same needle size and match the gauge. See the swatch on page 111.

DESIGNED BY LINDA LA BELLE

This hat matches the Confetti Sweater on page 108.

instructions

With CC B and the circular needle, cast on 72 (78, 84) sts. Join, being careful not to twist.

Work in k1, p1 ribbing for 1" (2.5cm).

Switch to MC yarn and knit in the round until the hat measures 4½ (5, 5½) (11.5 [12.5, 14]cm) from the cast-on edge.

decrease

Note You will stop decreasing when you have a total of 6 stitches remaining.

Rnd 1 *K10 (11, 12), k2tog*; repeat from * to * to end of round (66 [72, 78] sts).

Rnd 2 *K9 (10, 11), k2tog*; repeat from * to * to end of round (60 [66, 72] sts).

Rnd 3 *K8 (9, 10), k2tog*; repeat from * to * to end of round (54 [60, 66] sts).

Rnd 4 *K7 (8, 9), k2tog*, repeat from * to * to end of round (48 [54, 60] sts).

Switch to double-pointed needles.

Rnd 5 *K6 (7, 8), k2tog*; repeat from * to * to end of round (42 [48, 54] sts).

Rnd 6 *K5 (6, 7), k2tog*; repeat from * to * to end of round (36 [42, 48] sts).

Rnd 7 *K4 (5, 6), k2tog*; repeat from * to * to end of round (30 [36, 42] sts).

Rnd 8 *K3 (4, 5), k2tog*; repeat from * to * to end of round (24 [30, 36] sts).

Switch to CC D and continue as follows:

Rnd 9 *K2 (3, 4), k2tog*; repeat from * to * to end of round (18 [24, 30] sts).

Rnd 10 *K1 (2, 3), k2tog*; repeat from * to * to end of round (12 [18, 24] sts).

Sizes 6 months to 1 year and Toddler only * K1 (2), k2tog*; repeat from * to * to end of round (12 [18] sts).

Size Toddler only *K1, k2tog*; repeat from * to * to end of round (12 sts).

All Sizes K2tog around (6 sts).

top knot

There should be 6 stitches remaining on 3 needles (2 per needle). Work even on all stitches for 3" (7.5cm).

finishing

Cut a long tail, thread a tapestry needle, and run it through the remaining stitches.

Weave in the ends. Tie the "stem" into a knot.

THIS PAGE, CLOCKWISE FROM TOP: The yarn "Elaine" in colorway "Eleanor Roosevelt" freshly dyed and drying in the sun. Yarn on cones waiting to be made into skeins for dyeing. Hollyhocks in bloom. Skeined yarn ready for the dyepot. A day lily in one of Cheryl's many gardens. OPPOSITE PAGE: Cheryl Schaefer peeks over a bin of "Anne," her very popular sock yarn.

"There are no dye police."

CHERYL SCHAEFER, SCHAEFER YARN

At 6 in the morning, excited for my first interview for the book, I packed the rental car with snacks, a camera, a tape recorder, and my dog, Barley. I thought she would enjoy a trip to the country, and I wanted a little company on the five-hour drive to Interlaken, a small town in the Finger Lakes region in northern New York state. During the drive, I was chased by stormy weather, but on this hilltop, the home of Schaefer Yarn, the sun was brightly shining—it was a riot of color!

The home of Schaefer Yarn is surrounded by Cheryl's colorful gardens, and I could immediately see what a strong influence her environment has on her. The building that has housed Schaefer Yarn for the past fourteen years is also the home of Cheryl and her husband, Erich. They are building a new home up the hill, and Cheryl told me no yarn would be allowed in their new home. I could understand why—every inch of space in their current house has been taken over by the business, even through several expansions.

The company has nine full-time and six-part time employees, but when they started out it was only Cheryl and Erich doing all the work. Because the business is in their home, from 8 to 5 the Schaefers have little privacy. As Cheryl confided to me, she and her husband can't even have a spat. So it is time that they have a little space for themselves.

In good weather, the yarns hang out in the yard to dry. If the weather is bad, the yarns dry in the small barn where the yarn on cones gets skeined up prior to being dyed.

Cheryl and I went outside and sat under a beautiful old tree to talk. First I

had to get Barley, my dog, to settle down. My very citified dog would have climbed up on top of Cheryl's head if she could have. She was so overwhelmed by the numerous smells, new noises, and tickly grass, she first climbed up into Cheryl's lap, then tried to keep going up! Thank goodness Cheryl is an animal lover!

Cheryl discovered fiber while studying law at the University of California, Los Angeles. She took a fiber arts class that changed her life. For a period of time she made wall hangings from sisal, a stiff fiber used in rope making. On a visit to Israel, Cheryl went shopping and came across some handpainted yarn. Thinking to import this yarn to sell in California, she purchased some samples and waited for the order to arrive. Much to her disappointment, the yarn in the package did not match the samples. She thought to herself, I can do this and do it better!

Cheryl's career of dyeing yarn commercially began twenty-six years

ago in Northern California. She was a single parent of a disabled daughter living in Mendocino, California, when she decided to move east. She packed her car with yarns she had dyed and stopped to sell her yarns as she drove across the country. Through this, Cheryl built relationships with yarn stores that continue today. She spent nine years in New York City before moving with her now husband to Interlaken in 1992 and starting Schaefer Yarn. Today her daughter lives an independent life nearby.

The fibers are all natural—wool, silk, cotton, and mohair. Cheryl tries to get many of her yarns from American mills, but that is getting harder and harder these days. The dyes are low-impact acid dyes for wools and silks, and fiber reactive dyes on cottons. When all the dyeing is done there is still dye left in the jars and, caring for the environment, Cheryl did not want to pour this dye down the sink. So, she came up with Anne, a sock yarn, named for her

■ **interview** *(continued)*

friend Anne Niles Davenport, who is a quilter. These beautiful one-of-kind skeins use up all the leftover dye.

Cheryl has color memory, so if she sees a color she can jot down a note and is able to re-create the sense of that color. She sees color every-where—the reflection in a pond, a bug, a photo in a magazine, a person passing on the street.

Why is her business successful? Slow growth, an amazing color sense, and a true passion for what she does combined with respect for her employ-ees, the environment, and her craft. Cheryl also understands that creativity mustn't stop in the dye room. You must also be creative in business. One of the things she did that has worked so well was to name the colors of her yarns after memorable women. Each color has a brief bio—some names are easily recognized, such as Frida Kahlo, and others are more obscure, such as Chinese Empress Wu Zhao. Cheryl told me that people often write to her with suggestions for new names to add to the ever-growing list.

Her advice to the new dyer: Don't be afraid to try—"there are no dye police." If Cheryl had been afraid to try, Schaefer Yarn would never have come into existence. "Don't start out with your favorite or the most expensive yarn in your stash," she says. "Get something inexpensive, and then put down some color. Use fewer colors initially; don't use everything at once—everything leads to brown or gray. But you can always overdye."

Erich has retired from the business now and is overseeing the building of their new home. Cheryl is preparing her employees to take over the busi-ness when she retires someday in the future. She is looking forward to spending more time in her gardens and beginning all the projects she has been stashing fabric for.

Cheryl's work gives her great pleasure, equating the dyeing she does with her gardening; in the end you have something beautiful to show for your labor.

As I got ready to leave, both Schaefers filled my arms with wonder-ful gifts. Erich gave me handpicked tomatoes from the neighbor's garden and Cheryl showered me with plants from her garden and, of course, a skein of yarn!

And, just in case you are wondering, Barley was very relieved to put her paws down on the sidewalks of Brooklyn.

CLOCKWISE FROM UPPER LEFT: The home of Schaefer Yarn. Yarns on the outdoor drying rack. Laura Nelkin in the stockroom. Cheryl in one of her many gardens. "Anne," Schaefer Yarn's one-of-a-kind sock yarn. Erich Schaefer, bringing me a gift of handpicked tomatoes from a neighbor's garden. "Sandra" yarn packed and ready to ship.

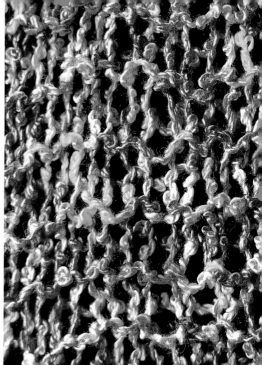

7

PRO washfast acid dyes

PRO WashFast Acid dyes are easy to use and come in a wide color range as well as kits. For the first project I picked a color directly from the jar, but for the other two projects in this chapter I decided to use the Summertime Sampler Kit and the Autumn Sampler kit.

PRO washfast immersion–dyed silk

MATERIALS

- **2 skeins Silk Chenille from Treenways Silks, 3¹/₂ oz (100g), 371 yds (339m), reskeined into 4 60" (150cm) skeins**
- **1 skein DMC Medicis Wool (Art. 475) Ecru**
- **Synthrapol**
- **Pro WashFast Acid Dye, #367 Watermelon**
- **Noniodized salt**
- **Citric acid**
- **Distilled white vinegar**

TOOLS

- **1 4-gal (16L) stainless steel or enamel pot**
- **Measuring cups**
- **Mixing spoon**
- **Measuring spoons**
- **Timer**

When Rachel DeNys and I first sat down to work out the Lacy Cardigan (page 122), I envisioned it in springtime pink. When I was testing the PRO WashFast Acid Dyes, I came across their Watermelon color, and I immediately knew that this was the color I wanted for the silk chenille yarn.

The yarn already comes in a skein, but I found the skein too dense to dye easily (the outside yarns grabbed all the color and the inside stayed white!), so I recommend that you ball up the skein and then split that ball into two 60" (150cm) skeins. Another option is to retie the figure 8s. Stretch the skein out under tension, find the original figure 8s, and with new yarn retie loosely where the original figure 8s were, then cut the originals out.

Another surprise that was in store for me was the reaction of the yarn to heat and water—the chenille wormed or folded back on itself, causing small areas of resistance

that did not take the dye. This was one of those moments that make you stop and realize you sometimes just have to listen to the yarn. I had pictured an evenly dyed yarn, but here I had something very different, and I really liked the effect—it added a new dimension to what I had in my mind's eye, and when knitted gave subtle highlights to the color, making the feeling even more summery!

I also found that the silk chenille was not appropriate for sewing up the lace jacket, so I dyed a matching yarn just for sewing the seams—DMC's Medicis Wool in Ecru. I used this same yarn to make the loop for the button.

prepare the yarn

1. In a dishpan, soak the yarn in 4 qt (4L) warm water, 110°F (44°C), with ¹/₂ tsp (2.5mL) Synthrapol for 1 hour.

prepare the dyestock

2. Mix ½ tsp (2g) dye powder with ½ cup (120mL) boiling water in a Pyrex container, stir thoroughly, and set aside for 1 hour.

prepare the dyebath

3. Place 2 gal (7.5L) room temperature water into the pot. Add the dissolved dyestock, ½ tbsp (7g) salt, ½ tsp (2.5mL) Synthrapol, and ½ tbsp (7g) citric acid. Stir well.

add the yarn

4. Remove the skeins from the soak solution and gently squeeze out excess water. Carefully shake out the skeins, and add all 4 silk chenille skeins and the DMC wool to the dyebath at the same time. Stir gently for 5 minutes to evenly distribute the dye.

5. Gradually raise the temperature of the dyebath to 185° (85°C), then maintain this temperature for 60 minutes, stirring occasionally. Caution: Do not go above this temperature—the silk chenille is delicate.

6. If at the end of 60 minutes your dyebath has not exhausted, slowly add 6½ tbsp (100mL) vinegar while holding the yarn out of the way. Maintain the temperature for an additional 10 minutes.

7. Allow the dye to cool completely in the dyepot before removing.

remove the yarn

8. Gently squeeze out the excess water and air dry. Once the yarn is dry, stretch the skeins back out and wind them into balls.

STEP 4

STEP 4 (CONTINUED)

STEP 5

STEP 6

lacy cardigan

DESIGNED BY RACHEL DE NYS AND LINDA LA BELLE

Rachel got her inspiration for the lace pattern from Barbara Walker, adapting the Vine Lace pattern from *A Treasury of Knitting Patterns*. The style of the cardigan was inspired by kimonos, which are constructed from a series of rectangles.

instructions

Tip If you knit the first and last stitch on each purl row, seaming the garment will be much easier.

back

Using the US #6 (4mm) needles, cast on 97 sts.

Work 6 rows in garter stitch.

Row 7 K7, yo, k2, ssk, k2tog, k2, *yo, k3, yo, k2, ssk, k2tog, k2*; repeat from * to * 5 times, yo, k3, yo, k2, ssk, k2tog, k2, yo, k5.

Row 8 Purl.

Row 9 K6, yo, k2, ssk, k2tog, k2, yo, *k3, yo, k2, ssk, k2tog, k2, yo*; repeat from * to * 5 times, k3, yo, k2, ssk, k2tog, k2, yo, k6.

Row 10 Purl.

Repeat Rows 7–10 24 more times (106 rows).

Work 6 rows in stockinette stitch (112 rows).

Row 113 K32, bind off 33 sts using the US #7 (4.5mm) needle, k32. Place all live stitches on 2 stitch holders.

sleeve (make 2)

Using the US #6 (4mm) needles, cast on 86 sts.

Work 6 rows in garter stitch.

Row 7 K7, yo, k2, ssk, k2tog, k2, *yo, k3, yo, k2, ssk, k2tog, k2*; repeat from * to * 4 times, yo, k3, yo, k2, ssk, k2tog, k2, yo, k5.

Row 8 Purl.

Row 9 K6, yo, k2, ssk, k2tog, k2, yo, *k3, yo, k2, ssk, k2tog, k2, yo*; repeat from * to * 4 times, k3, yo, k2, ssk, k2tog, k2, yo, k6.

Row 10 Purl.

Repeat Rows 7–10 25 more times (110 rows).

Work 4 rows in stockinette stitch (114 rows).

Bind off all stitches using the US #10 (6mm) needles.

Abbreviations & Techniques

k2tog Knit 2 stitches together.

k3tog Knit 3 stitches together.

ssk (slip, slip, knit) Slip the first 2 stitches from the left needle as if to knit. Insert the tip of the left needle in the front through both slipped stitches. Wrap the yarn around the tip of the right needle, and then knit these two stitches together.

sssk (slip, slip, slip, knit) Slip the first 3 stitches from the left needle as if to knit. Insert the tip of the left needle in the front through the 3 slipped stitches. Wrap the yarn around the tip of the right needle, and then knit these three stitches together.

yo (yarn over) This is simply the act of bringing the yarn forward as if to purl, then following your pattern. For this pattern, after your yarn over, it calls for you to k1 or ssk. So bring your yarn forward as if to purl, now you will either knit the first stitch on your left needle, or slip the first stitch from your left needle (see ssk). You will notice that the working yarn comes back over the top of your needle from the front of your work. This is correct. It will create another stitch on your needle (an increase), and what looks like a hole in your work (the lacy open stitch).

right front

Using the US #6 (4mm) needles, cast on 53 sts.

Work 6 rows in garter stitch.

Row 7 K7, yo, k2, ssk, k2tog, k2, *yo, k3, yo, k2, ssk, k2tog, k2*; repeat from * to * once, yo, k3, yo, k2, ssk, k2tog, k2, yo, k5.

Row 8 Purl.

Row 9 K6, yo, k2, ssk, k2tog, k2, yo, *k3, yo, k2, ssk, k2tog, k2, yo*; repeat from * to * once, k3, yo, k2, ssk, k2tog, k2, yo, k6.

Row 10 Purl.

Repeat Rows 7–10 10 more times. Repeat Rows 7 and 8 again (46 rows of lace pattern; 52 rows total).

decrease

Row 53 K4, ssk, yo, k2, ssk, k2tog, k2, yo, *k3, yo, k2, ssk, k2tog, k2, yo*; repeat from * to * once, k3, yo, k2, ssk, k2tog, k2, yo, k6 (52 sts).

Row 54 and all wrong side rows Purl.

Row 55 K4, ssk, yo, k2, ssk, k2tog, k2, *yo, k3, yo, k2, ssk, k2tog, k2*; repeat from * to * once, yo, k3, yo, k2, ssk, k2tog, k2, yo, k5 (51 sts).

Row 57 K4, k2, ssk, k2tog, k2, yo *k3, yo, k2, ssk, k2tog, k2, yo*; repeat from * to * once, k3, yo, k2, ssk, k2tog, k2, yo, k6 (50 sts).

Row 59 K6, ssk, k2tog, k2, *yo, k3, yo, k2, ssk, k2tog, k2*; repeat from * to * once, yo, k3, yo, k2, ssk, k2tog, k2, yo, k5 (49 sts).

Row 61 K4, ssk, k2tog, k2, yo, *k3, yo, k2, ssk, k2tog, k2, yo* repeat from * to * once, k3, yo, k2, ssk, k2tog, k2, yo, k6 (48 sts).

Row 63 K4, ssk, k2tog, k2 *yo, k3, yo, k2, ssk, k2tog, k2*; repeat from * to * once, yo, k3, yo, k2, ssk, k2tog, k2, yo, k5 (47 sts).

Row 65 K4, ssk, k2tog, yo, *k3, yo, k2, ssk, k2tog, k2, yo*; repeat from * to * once, k3, yo, k2, ssk, k2tog, k2, yo, k6 (46 sts).

Row 67 K4, ssk, k2tog, *yo, k3, yo, k2, ssk, k2tog, k2*; repeat from * to * once, yo, k3, yo, k1, k2tog, k5 (43 sts).

Row 69 K4, ssk, *k3, yo, k2, ssk, k2tog, k2, yo*; repeat from * to * once, k3, yo, k2, ssk, k2tog, k2, yo, k6 (44 sts).

Row 71 K4, ssk, k3, yo, k2, ssk, k2tog, k2, yo, k3, yo, k2, ssk, k2tog, k2, yo, k3, yo, k2, ssk, k2tog, k2, yo, k5 (43 sts).

☐ KNIT
⊡ PURL
◩ SSK
◪ K2 TOG
⊚ YARN OVER

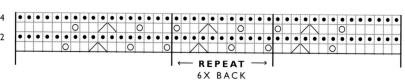

←— **REPEAT** —→
6X BACK
5X SLEEVES
2X FRONTS

Row 73 K4, ssk, k1, yo, k2, ssk, k2tog, k2, yo, k3, yo, k2, ssk, k2tog, k2, yo, k3, yo, k2, ssk, k2tog, k2, yo, k6 (42 sts).

Row 75 K4, ssk, k1, yo, k2, ssk, k2tog, k2, yo, k3, yo, k2, ssk, k2tog, k2, yo, k3, yo, k2, ssk, k2tog, k2, yo, k5 (41 sts).

Row 77 K7, ssk, k2tog, k2, yo, k3, yo, k2, ssk, k2tog, k2, yo, k3, yo, k2, ssk, k2tog, k2, yo, k6 (40 sts).

Row 79 K4, ssk, k1, yo, ssk, k2tog, k2, yo, k3, yo, k2, ssk, k2tog, k2, yo, k3, yo, k2, ssk, k2tog, k2, yo, k5 (39 sts).

Row 81 K5, ssk, k2tog, k2, yo, k3, yo, k2, ssk, k2tog, k2, yo, k3, yo, k2, ssk, k2tog, k2, yo, k6 (38 sts).

Row 83 K5, ssk, k2tog, k2, yo, k3, yo, k2, ssk, k2tog, k2, yo, k3, yo, k2, ssk, k2tog, k2, yo, k5 (37 sts).

Row 85 K4, ssk, k2tog, k1, yo, k3, yo, k2, ssk, k2tog, k2, yo, k3, yo, k2, ssk, k2tog, k2, yo, k6 (36 sts).

Row 87 K4, ssk, k2tog, k1, yo, k3, yo, k2, ssk, k2tog, k2, yo, k3, yo, k2, ssk, k2tog, k2, yo, k5 (35 sts).

Row 89 K4, ssk, k4, yo, k2, ssk, k2tog, k2, yo, k3, yo, k2, ssk, k2tog, k2, yo, k6 (34 sts).

Row 91 K4, sssk, yo, k3, yo, k2, ssk, k2tog, k2, yo, k3, yo, k2, ssk, k2tog, k2, yo, k5 (33 sts).

Row 93 K4, ssk, k2, yo, k2, ssk, k2tog, k2, yo, k3, yo, k2, ssk, k2tog, k2, yo, k6 (32 sts).

Row 95 K4, ssk, k4, yo, k2, ssk, k2tog, k2, yo, k3, yo, k2, ssk, k2tog, k2, yo, k5 (32 sts).

Row 97 K7, yo, k2, ssk, k2tog, k2, yo, k3, yo, k2, ssk, k2tog, k2, yo, k6 (32 sts).

Row 98 Purl.

Repeat Rows 95–98 twice (106 rows).

Work 6 rows in stockinette stitch (112 rows).

shoulder

Work the three-needle bind-off to make the right shoulder seam as follows: From the Back, slip the 32 right shoulder stitches onto a third needle. Holding the right (knit) sides of the Front and Back right shoulders together with the two needles parallel, slip an empty US #7 (4.5mm) needle into the first stitch on both needles and knit the two stitches as if they are one. Repeat so that you have two stitches on the right-hand needle. Pass the first stitch over the second stitch and off the needle. Continue in this manner until you have one stitch remaining on the right hand needle. Cut a long tail, and pass the tail through that stitch.

left front

Using the US #6 (4mm) needles, cast on 53 sts.

Work 6 rows in garter stitch.

invisible weaving This technique makes an invisible seam for stockinette stitch projects. Place the pieces next to each other and right side up on a flat surface. Thread your tapestry needle.

When you begin, leave approximately a 4" (10cm) tail of yarn; you will weave this in when you are finished sewing up the seam. Starting at the bottom of your seam, in the first full stitch in from the edge, *insert the needle under the ladder (horizontal bar). Next, insert the needle under the ladder on the other piece. Pull the yarn through, being careful to pull in the direction of the seam and not toward yourself*. Repeat from * to * until you have finished the seam. Weave in the ends.

SIMPLE YARN SUBSTITUTION

If you don't want to dye the yarn yourself, Treenway Silks can dye this yarn for you in your choice of 100 colors.

Row 7 K6, yo, k2, ssk, k2tog, k2, *yo, k3, yo, k2, ssk, k2tog, k2*; repeat from * to * once. Yo, k3, yo, k2, ssk, k2tog, k2, yo, k6.

Row 8 Purl.

Row 9 K5, yo, k2, ssk, k2tog, k2, yo, *k3, yo, k2, ssk, k2tog, k2, yo*; repeat from * to * once. K3, yo, k2, ssk, k2tog, k2, yo, k7.

Row 10 Purl.

Repeat Rows 7–10 10 more times. Repeat Rows 7 and 8 again. (46 rows of lace pattern; 52 rows total)

decrease

Row 53 K5, yo, k2, ssk, k2tog, k2, yo, *k3, yo, k2, ssk, k2tog, k2, yo*; repeat from * to * once. K3, yo, k2, ssk, k2tog, k2, yo, k2tog, k5 (52 sts).

Row 54 and all wrong side rows Purl.

Row 55 K6, yo, k2, ssk, k2tog, k2, *yo, k3, yo, k2, ssk, k2tog, k2*; repeat from * to * once. Yo, k3, yo, k2, ssk, k2tog, k7 (51 sts).

Row 57 K5, yo, k2, ssk, k2tog, k2, yo, *k3, yo, k2, ssk, k2tog, k2, yo*; repeat from * to * once. K3, yo, k2, ssk, k2tog, k7 (50 sts).

Row 59 K6, yo, k2, ssk, k2tog, k2, *yo, k3, yo, k2, ssk, k2tog, k2*; repeat from * to * once. Yo, k3, yo, k2, ssk, k2tog, k5 (49 sts).

Row 61 K5, yo, k2, ssk, k2tog, k2, yo, *k3, yo, k2, ssk, k2tog, k2, yo*; repeat from * to * once. K3, yo, k2, ssk, k2tog, k5 (48 sts).

Row 63 K6, yo, k2, ssk, k2tog, k2, *yo, k3, yo, k2, ssk, k2tog, k2*; repeat from * to * once. Yo, k3, yo, k1, k3tog, k5 (47 sts).

Row 65 K5, yo, k2, ssk, k2tog, k2, yo, *k3, yo, k2, ssk, k2tog, k2, yo*; repeat from * to * once. K3, yo, k1, k3tog, k5 (46 sts).

Row 67 K6, yo, k2, ssk, k2tog, k2, *yo, k3, yo, k2, ssk, k2tog, k2*; repeat from * to * once. Yo, k3, k2tog, k5 (45 sts).

Row 69 K5, yo, k2, ssk, k2tog, k2, yo, *k3, yo, k2, ssk, k2tog, k2, yo*; repeat from * to * once. K3, k2tog, k5 (44 sts).

Row 71 K6, yo, k2, ssk, k2tog, k2, *yo, k3, yo, k2, ssk, k2tog, k2*; repeat from * to * once. Yo, k1, k2tog, k5 (43 sts).

Row 73 K5, yo, k2, ssk, k2tog, k2, yo, *k3, yo, k2, ssk, k2tog, k2, yo*; repeat from * to * once. K1, k2tog, k5 (42 sts).

Row 75 K6, yo, k2, ssk, k2tog, k2, yo, k3, yo, k2, ssk, k2tog, k2, yo, k3, yo, k2, ssk, k2tog, k8 (41 sts).

Row 77 K5, yo, k2, ssk, k2tog, k2, yo, k3, yo, k2, ssk, k2tog, k2, yo, k3, yo, k2, ssk, k2tog, k8 (40 sts).

Row 79 K6, yo, k2, ssk, k2tog, k2, yo, k3, yo, k2, ssk, k2tog, k2, yo, k3, yo, k2, ssk, k2tog, k6 (39 sts).

Row 81 K5, yo, k2, ssk, k2tog, k2, yo, k3, yo, k2, ssk, k2tog, k2, yo, k3, yo, k2, ssk, k2tog, k6 (38 sts).

Row 83 K6, yo, k2, ssk, k2tog, k2, yo, k3, yo, k2, ssk, k2tog, k2, yo, k3, yo, k2, k3tog, k5 (37 sts).

Row 85 K5, yo, k2, ssk, k2tog, k2, yo, k3, yo, k2, ssk, k2tog, k2, yo, k3, yo, k2, k3tog, k5 (36 sts).

Row 88 K6, yo, k2, ssk, k2tog, k2, yo, k3, yo, k2, ssk, k2tog, k2, yo, k3, k1, k2tog, k5 (35 sts).

Row 89 K5, yo, k2, ssk, k2tog, k2, yo, k3, yo, k2, ssk, k2tog, k2, yo, k4, k2tog, k5 (34 sts).

Row 91 K6, yo, k2, ssk, k2tog, k2, yo, k3, yo, k2, ssk, k2tog, k2, yo, k2, k2tog, k5 (33 sts).

Row 93 K5, yo, k2, ssk, k2tog, k2, yo, k3, yo, k2, ssk, k2tog, k2, yo, k2, k2tog, k5 (32 sts).

Row 95 K6, yo, k2, ssk, k2tog, k2, yo, k3, yo, k2, ssk, k2tog, k2, yo, k7 (32 sts).

Row 97 K5, yo, k2, ssk, k2tog, k2, yo, k3, yo, k2, ssk, k2tog, k2, yo, k8 (32 sts).

Row 98 Purl.

Repeat Rows 95-98 twice (106 rows).

Work 6 rows in stockinette stitch (112 rows).

shoulder

Work the three-needle bind-off to make the left shoulder seam as follows: From the Back, slip the 32 left shoulder stitches onto a third needle. Holding the right (knit) sides of the Front and Back right shoulders together with the two needles parallel, slip an empty US #7 (4.5mm) needle into the first stitch on both needles and knit the two stitches as if they are one. Repeat so that you have two stitches on the right-hand needle. Pass the first stitch over the second stitch and off the needle. Continue in this manner until you have one stitch remaining on the right hand needle. Cut a long tail, and pass the tail through that stitch.

finishing

Block the sleeves and body of the cardigan before sewing together. Block the sleeves to 8" x 14" (20.5cm x 35.5cm). Lay the back and attached fronts out flat to form one rectangle 19" x 30" (48cm x 76cm). Allow to dry flat.

Using the DMC Medicis Wool, sew the top of the sleeves to the body, centering them at the shoulder seam and ending 7 1/2" (19cm) down from the shoulder seam. Now sew the side and sleeve seams in one long seam, using the invisible weaving technique. Weave in any loose ends.

Make the loop for the button. Using the DMC Medicis Wool doubled and size D-3 (3.25mm) crochet hook, join the yarn on the Right Front 3/8" (1cm) below the beginning of the neckline decrease. Chain 12, join to the body of the cardigan 3/8" (1cm) above the starting point with a slip stitch. Weave in the ends. Sew a 3/8" (1cm) button on the left front.

PRO washfast handpainted silk

MATERIALS

- **1 oz (28 g) Tiara 100% Silk Boucle from Henry's Attic**
- **Citric acid**
- **Synthrapol**
- **PRO WashFast Acid Dye Summertime Sampler**
- **Distilled white vinegar**

TOOLS

- **Dust mask**
- **Gloves**
- **Enamel or stainless steel pot**
- **Measuring spoons**
- **Measuring cups**
- **Small whisks**
- **Plastic wrap**
- **6 1" (2.5cm) sponge brushes**
- **6 small (¹/₂ cup [120mL]) containers with lids**
- **Metal muffin tin to hold the containers**
- **12" (30cm) ruler**
- **Vegetable steamer**

The yarn for this project, Tiara Silk Boucle, is the same as the yarn used in the City Streets project (page 86). I wanted you to see what happens when you take the same yarn, two different dye products, and two different dye methods—painting along the length of the skein and painting across the width of the skein. You'll discover that when knitted up, there is a difference in how the color lays.

There's no thickener in this dye recipe, so be cautious as you paint, being sure to leave white space around each color.

The color order I chose makes the yarn red-dominant; feel free to vary the color order to your liking.

prepare the yarn

1. In a dishpan, soak the yarn in 2 qt (2L) warm water (110°F [44°C]), 3 tbsp

STEP 4

STEP 5

STEP 6

(15mL) citric acid, and 1/2 tsp (2.5mL) Synthrapol for 1 hour.

prepare the dyestock

2. Mark the containers with the names of the colors to avoid confusion. Put on your dust mask and gloves. For each of the colors, make a paste of 1/2 tsp (2g) dye powder with a small amount of boiling water. Then add enough boiling water to make to 1/2 cup (120mL) of stock, and set aside to cool for 1 hour.

paint the yarn

3. While wearing protective gloves, remove the skein from the soak solution and lay on plastic wrap in an open oval.

4. As you paint the skein, be sure to mop up any pools of color that accumulate on the plastic wrap! Using a sponge brush and the Watermelon dye, about 6" (15cm) from the beginning of the skein, paint a 2" (5cm) wide area across the width of the skein. Repeat around the skein.

5. With the side of the brush, paint a narrow strip of Sea Breeze across the width of the skein, centered between the Watermelon brush strokes.

6. Make an approximately 1" (2.5cm) high and 1" (2.5cm) wide dab of Key Lime on either side of the Sea Breeze stroke on only one edge of the skein.

7. On the opposite edge of the skein, make short dabs with Cantaloupe to the left of the Sea Breeze stroke. Staying on the same edge of the skein, make short dabs with Sun Yellow to the right of the Sea Breeze stroke.

8. The last color you will put on the skein is Iris. Look the skein over and use the Iris to fill in any wide gaps, being careful to leave white space—it may be just a tiny dab here and there.

9. Mop up any pools of color. Lay plastic wrap over the skein (you may need to overlap two pieces), then seal the middle and the edges.

10. Fold the packet in half lengthwise, roll, and allow the yarn to rest for at least 15 minutes before steaming. I find that this allows for better color saturation.

steam the yarn

11. Place water and a vegetable steamer in the pot. (The water should not touch the bottom of the vegetable steamer.) Place the coiled up skein on top of the vegetable steamer. (I like to remove the little post; simply unscrew it to remove it.)

12. Steam for 30 minutes, starting the timer only once the water begins to boil. Do not let the water boil away.

13. Turn off the heat and allow the yarn to cool completely in the pot (this may take several hours). This is very important: You will get better color and better adherence of the dyestuff.

remove the yarn

14. Remove the plastic wrap. Never attempt to open a hot, plastic-wrapped packet of yarn; the steam could burn you!

15. Rinse thoroughly in warm water. Allow the yarn to air dry. Once the skein is dry, stretch it back out and wind into a ball.

STEP 7

STEP 8

STEP 9

springtime scarf

DESIGNED BY LINDA LA BELLE

This is a quick and easy scarf that looks great with jeans, or it can be dressy! I recommend that you cast on and bind off on a needle at least 2 sizes larger.

instructions

Using larger needles, cast on 22 stitches. Switch to smaller needles and knit every row until you have 36" (91.5cm) of yarn left.

Bind off with the larger needle.

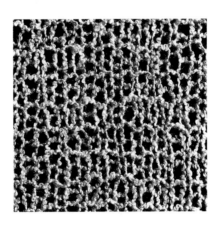

SIMPLE YARN SUBSTITUTION

If you would like to make this scarf but do not want to go to the trouble of dyeing your yarn, HABU Textiles has a beautiful silk boucle, #A-5 1/5 Kusaki Zome, naturally dyed, 100% silk, 1 1/2 oz (42g), 233 yds (213m). It will knit up in a similar texture using a US #8 (5mm) needle and 22 stitches. The sample swatch was knit up in color #36.

PRO washfast handpainted wool

MATERIALS

- **2 skeins Thirteen Mile Farm Thick and Thin Bulky, 100% organic wool, 4 oz (113g), 64 yd (58m), color Oatmeal**
- **Synthrapol**
- **Citric acid**
- **PRO WashFast Acid Dye Autumn Sampler, with colors Turkey Red, Evergreen, Purple, Spiced Pumpkin, Maple Sugar, Mochachino**
- **Distilled white vinegar**

TOOLS

- **Dust mask**
- **Gloves**
- **Enamel or stainless steel pot**
- **Measuring spoons**
- **Measuring cups**
- **Small whisks**
- **Plastic wrap**
- **6 1" (2.5cm) sponge brushes**
- **6 small (1/2 cup [125mL]) containers with lids**
- **Metal muffin tin to hold the containers**
- **12" (30cm) ruler**
- **Vegetable steamer**

Earlier (page 128) we worked with the PRO WashFast Acid dyes on silk, and now we are going to try them out on wool. The wool for this project came from Thirteen Mile Farm. You can find out more about Thirteen Mile Farm in my interview with Becky Weed on page 138.

The wool is a blend of Corriedale, Columbia, Corriedale/Border Leicester cross, and Romeldale sheep. For many of the projects in this book we have been dyeing over white or ecru yarn. I wanted to show you how rich the colors could be when you dye over a natural light gray yarn. Because we are doing a winter hat, I chose the PRO WashFast Acid Dye Autumn Sampler. How can you resist, with color names like Maple Sugar and Spiced Pumpkin? I decided to make Turkey Red the dominant color for this project; the colors came out so saturated!

prepare the yarn

1. In a dishpan, make a soak solution of 1 tsp (5mL) Synthrapol, 3 tbsp (43g) citric acid, and 4 qt (4L) warm water [110°F (44°C)]. This solution can be stored in a closed container and kept indefinitely for reuse to soak more yarn.

2. Rewind the skein into an 8 yd (7.3m) diameter skein. In a dishpan, soak the skein in the soak solution for 1 hour.

prepare the dyestock

3. Label six separate 1/2 cup (120mL) containers with the dye colors. Place 1/2 tsp (2g) dye powder in each container and make into a paste with a small amount of boiling water. Add enough boiling water to equal 1/2 cup (120mL). Set the dyestocks aside for 1 hour. Any leftover dyestock can be stored covered for a minimum of six months.

paint the yarn

4. Wearing rubber gloves, remove your skein from the soak solution and squeeze out any excess water. Place the skein on the plastic wrap in an oval.

5. Because the yarn is so thick, paint only one or two strands at a time along the length of the skein. The brush strokes should vary in length: the longest for the dominant color (Turkey Red) and the shortest for the accent color (Mochachino). This dyestock has not been thickened, so be sure to leave a little of the substrate showing. This makes for a more interesting yarn and allows for bleeding without the likelihood of colors blending and turning muddy. Following the photographs, first paint with Turkey Red, picking up two strands and painting 6" (15cm), leave about a 12" (30cm) space, and repeat on the top edge of the skein. At the bottom edge, in the open space between the two painted areas on the top, paint a 6" (15cm) stroke of Turkey Red on two strands of yarn. Repeat around the skein.

6. Evergreen is next; come down from the top of the skein a bit and begin about an inch in from the end of the Turkey Red stripe. Pick up two or three strands and paint a 5" (12.5cm) section. Repeat this around, painting under the Turkey Red stripes on the top edge of the skein only.

7. Time for Purple: At the bottom edge of the skein paint a 4" (10cm) stripe, picking up two or three strands to the left of the Turkey Red stripe on the bottom of the skein. Repeat around the skein.

STEP 5

STEP 6

STEP 7

STEP 8

STEP 9

STEP 10

STEP 11

8. With Spiced Pumpkin, pick up a couple of strands and paint a 3" (7.5cm) stripe, starting under the Evergreen stripe and painting the stroke to the right. Repeat around.

9. With Maple Sugar, paint a 2" (5cm) stripe in the center of the opening at the top of the skein between the two Turkey

Red stripes.

10. Use the Mochachino as an accent color—fill in any gaps, picking only one or two strands, and don't forget to leave white space!

11. Mop up any pools of color and place plastic wrap on top and carefully flip the skein over, touching up any areas where the color did not get through. Cover the skein with plastic wrap, sealing the center and then the outer edges. Leave the skein to sit for 15 minutes before steaming. You will notice that the color moves along the skein as it rests. Fold the skein in half and roll it up.

steam the yarn

12. Place water and a vegetable steamer in the pot. (The water should not touch the bottom of the vegetable steamer.) Place the coiled up skein on top of the

vegetable steamer. (I like to remove the little post; simply unscrew it to remove it.)

13. Steam for 30 minutes, starting the timer only once the water begins to boil. Do not let the water boil away.

14. Turn off the heat and allow the packet to cool completely in the pot This is very important. You will get better color and better adherence of the dyestuff.

remove the yarn

15. Remove the plastic wrap. Never attempt to open a hot, plastic-wrapped packet of yarn; the steam could burn you!

16. Rinse the yarn in warm water with ¼ tsp (1.25mL) Synthrapol, then rinse in clear water 2–3 times. Allow the yarn to air dry. Once the skeins is dry, stretch it back out and wind into a ball.

cat hat

DESIGNED BY LINDA LA BELLE

SKILL LEVEL
Intermediate

MATERIALS
- 2 skeins Thirteen Mile Farm Bulky Thick & Thin, 3½ oz (100g), 64 yds (58m)
- 1 16" (40.5cm) US #13 (9mm) circular needle
- 1 set 7" (18cm) US #13 (9mm) double-pointed needles
- stitch marker
- tapestry needle

GAUGE
- In stockinette stitch
- 6½ stitches and 11 rows = 3" (7.5cm)

SIZE
One size; approximately 20" (51cm) around

This hat came about at the request of one of my knitting students. She wanted a hat with catlike ears. I like to keep patterns simple, and I did not want to make the ears separately. I found that by doing a three-needle bind-off across the top of the hat, you have instant ears!

Abbreviations & Techniques

k2tog Knit two stitches together.

M1L (make 1 left) With tip of the left needle, lift the strand between the last stitch knitted and next stitch on left-hand needle from front to back. Knit into the back of it to increase 1 stitch.

M1R (make 1 right) With tip of the left needle, lift the strand between the last stitch knitted and next stitch on left-hand needle from back to front. Knit into the front of it to increase 1 stitch.

ssk (slip, slip, knit) Slip the first 2 stitches from the left needle as if to knit. Insert the tip of the left needle in the front through both slipped stitches. Wrap the yarn around the tip of the right needle, and then knit these two stitches together.

instructions

Cast on 27 stitches. Do not join.

Rows 1–4 Knit.

Row 5 K4, p19, k4.

Row 6 Knit.

Row 7 K4, p19, k4.

Row 8 Knit.

Row 9 K4, p19, k4.

Row 10 K13, M1L, k1, M1R, k13 (29 sts).

Row 11 K4, p21, k4.

Row 12 K13, M1L, k3, M1R, k13 (31 sts).

Row 13 K4, p23, k4.

Row 14 K13, M1L, k5, M1R, k13 (33 sts).

Row 15 K4, p25, k4.

Row 16 K13, M1L, k7, M1R, k13 (35 sts).

Row 17 K4, p27, k4.

Row 18 K13, M1L, k9, M1R, k13 (37 sts).

Row 19 K4, p29, k4.

Row 20 Knit to the end of the row. Turn, and cast on 12 stitches. Turn, and join with the yarn in front by slipping the last cast-on stitch from the right needle to the left. Place marker on the right hand needle, and p2tog (to join), p3, k29, p4, k11 (48 sts). Begin working in the round.

Rnd 1 and all odd-numbered rounds Knit.

Rnd 2 P4, k29, p4, ssk, k7, k2tog (46 sts).

Rnd 4 P4, k29, p4, k9.

Rnd 6 K4, k29, p4, ssk, k5, k2tog (44 sts).

Rnd 8 P4, k29, p4, k7.

Rnd 10 P4, k29, p4, ssk, k3, k2tog (42 sts).

Rnd 12 P4, k29, p4, k5

Rnd 14 P4, k29, p4, ssk, k1, k2tog (40 sts).

Rnd 16 P4, k29, p4, k3.

finishing

Work a three-needle bind-off as follows: Knit 9 stitches, turn the hat inside out, and slip 20 stitches to a double-pointed needle. The remaining 20 stitches can stay on the circular needle. Holding the two needles with the stitches parallel, slip an empty needle into both stitches as if to knit, and knit the two together. Repeat this step so that you have two stitches on your right hand needle. Bring the further stitch over and off the needle so that you are binding off 1 stitch.

Keep knitting the first stitch on both left hand needles together. Pass each further stitch over and off the needle, as a normal bind-off, until you have one stitch remaining on the right hand needle. Cut the yarn and pass the tail through that stitch.

Weave in the ends.

SIMPLE YARN SUBSTITUTION

If you fell in love with the Cat Hat but you do not wish to dye the yarn, I found the perfect substitution yarn. It is TNT from Chasing Rainbows Dyeworks, 100% wool, 3½ oz (100g), 140 yd (128m). We were able to keep the same needle size and match the gauge. The sample swatch for the TNT yarn is knit up in "New Blue."

■ interview

BECKY WEED, THIRTEEN MILE FARM

WITH KATEY PLYMESSER

Thirteen Mile Farm is located in Belgrade, Montana, in the Gallatin Valley at the base of the Bridger Mountains, an area filled with history and fertile land. On my first morning at the farm, it was gray and drizzling, and I was feeling out of place—it took me a while to figure out what was wrong. Here I was in the middle of a landscape of vast openness, not the overpopulated streets of Brooklyn, able to see for miles. Suddenly I realized that it was the openness that was affecting me, and I started to feel better. I hadn't expected the landscape to affect me in such a way.

Thirteen Mile Farm is a vertical operation, and that is what attracted me to it. Becky Weed and her husband, David Tyler, raise the sheep, have them shorn, clean the fleece, dye it with natural dyes, then pick it, card it, draft it, and spin it into yarn. They also sell meat from their lambs for eating. They have two employees, Kathryn (Katey) Plymesser and Melissa Stringham. What Becky and Dave do is pretty special and very labor intensive. They know that every step makes a difference in the final product.

They have been on the farm for twenty years—originally they only sold the meat; Becky thought to use the wool. After a bad experience of sending out the fiber to be processed, she thought, "I can do it better." And she has. It took a long time to get their wool processing operation up and running. These days, Melissa runs the equipment in the wool barn and Katey divides her time between the wool barn and the dye house.

Thirteen Mile Farm produces sportweight, worsted weight, and bulky yarns in five colors each. They can do custom yarns for people as long as it is ordered in sufficient quantity. The mill has spun a variety of sheep's wool, guanaco, alpaca, and llama. Their own flock is a mix of sheep breeds chosen first for the quality of meat they will produce and second for a long and lustrous fiber.

Their land is certified organic, and so are their grass-fed sheep. The wool is also certified organic, a product that is becoming more in demand.

Operations at the farm are definitely "green" in nature. Becky and Dave had just finished haying when I arrived. This hay will be the livestock's winter food. The water for processing the fleeces is heated by solar panels on the roof of the wool barn and the solution used to clean (scour) the fleece is a citrus-based product. The wastewater from the scouring process is then spread on the fields. Becky and Dave are part of a growing group of livestock farmers who believe in a predator-friendly philosophy. This means that they have made a commitment not to allow any lethal control (shooting, trapping, or poisoning) to protect their sheep from native predators. Instead, they protect their livestock through the use of good fencing, rotating the pastures where the sheep reside, three guard llamas, and Taiga, a border collie.

When I met Katey, she was new to dyeing on a large scale, but I was confident she would be very good at it. The day I was there she was dyeing with indigo (one of my favorite dyestuffs). My original interview with Katey is lost—the tape broke at 30,000 feet while traveling back from another interview. So I called her up and we talked again. Several months had passed, and there had been some changes.

Katey has begun dyeing the yarn rather than the fleece. She found it to

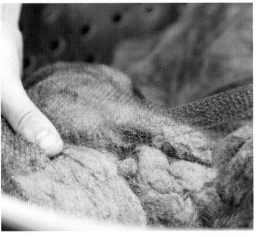

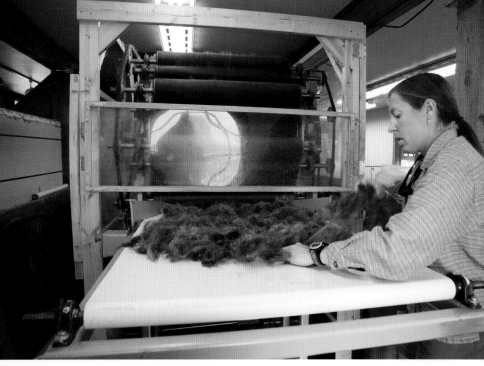

THIS PAGE, CLOCKWISE FROM TOP LEFT: Katey Plymesser lifts fiber out of the indigo pot. Cyrus, one of three guard Llamas, and a few of the flock on their way to the next pasture. Melissa Stringham at the carding machine; here she places the scoured fiber in position to be fed into the carder. The dyed fiber being spun into singles. Fiber oxidizing after coming out of the indigo pots. OPPOSITE PAGE, LEFT TO RIGHT: The John Reese Homestead, home of Becky Weed and Dave Tyler; it is a lovingly restored log home, circa 1865 (the trees are older than the house!). Goldenrod ready to harvest; once dry, this weed will be used to make a yellow dyestock.

THIS PAGE, CLOCKWISE FROM TOP LEFT: New solar panels on the barn roof; the water heated by these panels is used to scour the fleece. Fiber soaking in the indigo pot—the coppery scum is the sign of a successful indigo pot. Thirteen Mile Farm has a small shop, where the yarns are on display. Taiga, the ranch's border collie. Looking across the Gallatin Valley at the Bridger Mountain Range.
OPPOSITE PAGE, CLOCKWISE FROM TOP LEFT: Becky Weed sorts a fleece. The Bridger Mountains hiding behind low-lying clouds.

■ interview (*continued*)

be more efficient and easier on her physically, and it allows them to dye to order. Another factor was the time Katey and Melissa had to spend cleaning all the wool-processing equipment after sending through the dyed fiber.

Katey is a spinner, knitter, weaver, and also a crocheter. She had been dyeing at home as a hobby. Over time Katey began to help out at the farm with their events. It was at one of these events that Becky approached Katey to manage the wool mill. Becky wanted to use natural dyes, so she sent Katey off to a workshop with Michelle Wipplinger of Earthues in Seattle. In the four months since I first spoke with Katey she had become more confident, though she knows that there is much to learn. She told me her most favorite part of the process is spinning out the yarn in the washing machine, pressing stop, lifting the lid, and seeing the yarn at that stage. At 28, Katey is one of the youngest professional dyers I have come across.

She is enjoying what she is doing and feels it is a good challenge. As a former civil engineer working in land development, she now feels very good to be doing things that are not harming the land!

Becky and Katey plan on gathering dyestuff and in the future plant a dye garden. In the immediate vicinity there are chokecherries, sagebrush, goldenrod, and tansy, all of which could be used to color yarns. Becky sent me across the fields to get a look at a large growth of goldenrod they would be cutting down and using for yellow dye. I couldn't believe it; here I was, this city slicker, traipsing across the Montana plains at sunset! The smells were amazing, the sheep were baa-ing in the background, and the setting sun touched everything with the most beautiful golden light. This was a moment I never wanted to let go of.

At the end of the day, I sat with Becky and David in the living room of their log home, which had been built by homesteader John Reese in the late 1800s. Listening to them talk about the pioneers and Indians who had inhabited this valley so long ago, I could easily imagine the herds of bison walking across the plain. Watching the sunset over the Gallatin Valley, I realized that Becky and David are not just shepherds of their flock but shepherds of their land as well.

Becky's advice: "Try to understand what your own passions are. Figure out what your goals are: Do you want to try and make a living or is it just to have fun and be creative?" She stresses that both are legitimate and both are important.

Becky is passing the fiber side of the business on to Katey so that she can focus on raising the sheep and managing the grasses. Knowing that it is important to have balance in their lives, Becky and David try to be sure that they take time away to go to the mountains, hiking and canoeing in the summer and skiing in the winter.

Thirteen Mile Farm is proof that small-scale agriculture can work with a combination of commitment to the story behind the product and people caring about the quality of the product.

8

PRO one shot dyes

The PRO One Shot Dyes are another great dye product available in kit form. Everything you need is in the jar: It's no fuss, no muss. The kit comes with three primary colors; we will make three secondary colors from the stock for a total of six colors.

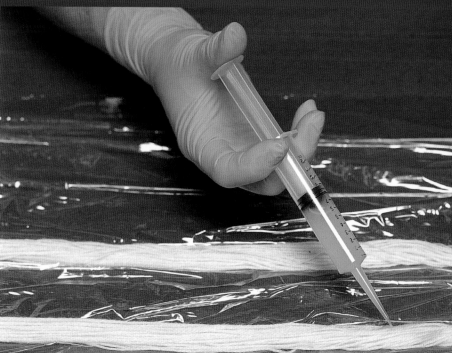

PRO one shot handpainted superwash merino wool/tencel

MATERIALS

- 3¹/₂ oz (100g), 360 yds (329m) 3-ply 50% superwash merino, 50% tencel, from Ashland Bay Trading Co.

- Synthrapol

- PRO One Shot Sampler, with colors Buttercup OS16, Cherry OS38, Cornflower OS41

- Jacquard Super Clear

TOOLS

- 9 ¹/₂-cup (120mL) containers

- Measuring cups

- Measuring spoons

- Tape measure

- Plastic wrap

- Acrylic yarn

- 3 1" (2.5cm) sponge brushes

- 4 syringes

- Vegetable steamer

Socks are one of my favorite things to knit, and what's more fun than a yarn that will self-stripe? Here's how to make your own self-striping yarn.

prepare the yarn

1. Reskein the yarn into 2 skeins 8²/₃ yds (7.9m) in diameter each. It is important that you make one skein, leave it on the tool, and then make the second above the first. When you do the figure 8s, run them through both skeins. I recommend that you use a different color yarn for the figure 8s at either end of the skein. Before removing the skeins, secure in several spots along the length with lark-shead knots to help keep it under control.

2. Place the skein in a dishpan with soak solution of 4 qt (4L) warm water [110°F (44°C)] and ¹/₂ tsp (2mL) Synthrapol. Soak for 1 hour.

prepare the dyestock

3. In each of three containers place 2¹/₂ tsp (12g) dye powder and form into a paste with a small amount of boiling water. Add more boiling water to equal ¹/₂ cup (120mL), stir well, and set aside to cool completely.

4. In each of three containers place 1¹/₂ tsp (7mL) Super Clear and the following:

   BLUE-GREEN: 1 fl. oz (30mL) Cornflower, ¹/₂ fl. oz (15mL) Buttercup

   RED-VIOLET: 1 fl. oz (30mL) Cornflower, ¹/₂ fl. oz (15mL) Cherry

   RED-ORANGE: 1 fl. oz (30mL) Cherry, ¹/₂ fl. oz (15mL) Buttercup

5. In another set of three containers, place 2 tsp (10mL) Super Clear and 2 fl. oz (60mL) of each stock color.

Be sure that you have marked each of the containers with the names of the colors—it is easy to get them confused.

paint the yarn

6. Remove the skein from the soak solution and gently squeeze out any excess water.

7. Find the beginning of the skein. Place this at the end of the worktable on top of plastic wrap, forming an oval. You may need to remove one or more of the larkshead knots to do this. You need to have 60" (152.5cm) of skein exposed (30" [76cm] on either side of the starting point) as shown. If you cannot lay the entire skein out on your table, place the remainder of the skein (still held with a larkshead knot) in a large ziplock bag to keep it moist. If you are able to lay out the entire skein, cover it to keep the skein moist.

8. As you paint the skein with the sponge brush, vary the pressure, which will give a slight variegation to your yarn. Starting with thickened Cornflower and a 1" (2.5cm) sponge brush, paint 30" (76cm) on either side of the start point for a total of 60" (152.5cm) as shown. Carefully turn this section over and paint other side. Flip it back over, mop up any excess dyestuff, and place plastic wrap on top, sealing the center and rolling up the painted section. Rinse any excess dyestuff off your gloved hands so that you do not spread dye to the unpainted yarn. Be sure to do this each time you finish a segment before you touch the undyed yarn.

9. Place more plastic wrap on the worktable and remove a 36" (91.5cm) segment from the ziplock bag, removing any larkshead knots and spreading the skein apart to maintain the oval.

10. Fill a syringe with the thickened Buttercup and randomly make syringe dots on top of the yarn. Carefully flip

STEP 1

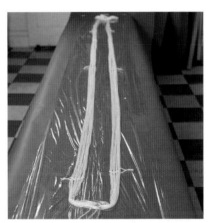

STEP 7

STEP 8

STEP 8 (CONTINUED)

STEP 8 (CONTINUED)

STEP 10

this section over and repeat on the other side. Mop up any excess dyestuff and flip it back over. Cover with plastic wrap to protect what you have just dyed. Do not roll up.

11. Fill another syringe with thickened cherry and repeat on the other 36" (91cm) segment. Cover this with plastic wrap, pressing down in the center so that the two segments cannot touch each other, and roll up.

12. Place more plastic wrap on the work table and remove a 60" (152.5cm) segment from the ziplock bag, removing any larkshead knots if needed and

spreading it apart to maintain the oval.

13. Using a 1" (2.5cm) sponge brush and the thickened Blue-Green dyestuff, paint the 60" (152.5cm) segment in front of the yellow dots, varying the pressure as you paint, flipping over to do the other side and flipping back. Cover with plastic wrap to protect what you have just dyed. Do not roll up.

14. Fill four syringes with the following colors: Red-Orange, Buttercup, Cornflower, Red-Violet. Make random color dots along the 60" (152.5cm) segment that is in front of the section with the red dots. Carefully flip over,

repeat, and flip back, mopping up any excess dyestuff. Cover this with plastic wrap, pressing down in the center so that the two segments cannot touch each other, and roll up.

15. Place more plastic wrap on the worktable and remove the final segment from the ziplock bag. Using a 1" (2.5cm) sponge brush and the thickened Red-Violet, paint this final section as before and cover in plastic wrap. Roll the entire skein up and allow to sit for 15 minutes.

steam the yarn

16. Place water and a vegetable steamer in the pot. (The water should not touch the bottom of the vegetable steamer.) Place the coiled up skein on top of the vegetable steamer. (Unscrew the post to remove it.)

17. Steam for 30 minutes, starting the timer only once the water begins to boil. Be sure the water does not evaporate—add more if necessary.

18. When the time is up, turn off the heat and allow the packet to cool completely in the pot. This is very important. You will get better color and better adherence of the dyestuff.

remove the yarn

19. Remove the plastic wrap. Never attempt to open a hot, plastic-wrapped packet of yarn; the steam could burn you!

20. Place the skeins in warm water with 1/4 tsp (1.25ml) Synthrapol, and let soak for a few minutes. Change the water several times, then remove the yarn and gently squeeze out any excess water. Allow the yarn to air dry.

21. Once the skeins are dry, stretch them back out under tension and wind into balls.

STEP 11

STEP 13

STEP 14

STEP 15

self-striping socks with roll cuff

DESIGNED BY SHANNON BROCK AND LINDA LA BELLE

SKILL LEVEL
Intermediate

MATERIALS
- 2 skeins 3-ply 50% Superwash Merino/50% Tencel Ashland Bay Trading Co., 1³/₄ oz (50g), 180 yds (165m) each
- 1 set US #2 (2.75mm) double-pointed needles
- 1 pair US #4 (3.5mm) straight needles, for casting on

GAUGE
- In stockinette stitch
- 30 stitches and 48 rows = 4" (10cm)

SIZE
Average woman's foot; approximately 8" (20.5cm) long and 8.5" (21.5cm) around ball of foot

Abbreviations & Techniques

k2tog Knit 2 stitches together.

knit pick up Insert the tip of the right-hand needle under the edge stitch, wrap the yarn, and pull the loop through

p2tog Purl 2 stitches together.

psso Pass the slipped stitch over.

In real life, Shannon is a papermaker. I am lucky to have her teaching at The Yarn Tree. Besides teaching felting and papermaking for me, she also teaches the sock and mitten classes. She really had fun with the yarn, and I love the simple pattern she came up with—it really allows the yarn to do the talking!

kitchener stitch The Kitchener stitch is used to join live stitches. The seam looks like a continuous row of stockinette stitch. It is important that you match the tension of the work; you do not want your seam to be too loose, nor too tight.

The live stitches need to be placed evenly on two needles, cutting the working yarn approximately 4 times the width of the work. Thread a tapestry needle with the working yarn. Hold the two needles together in your left hand with the right side (knit side) of the work facing out. Note: It does not matter if the working yarn is on the front needle or the back needle!

Begin using the tapestry needle, bring the working yarn through the first stitch on the front needle, going into the stitch as if to purl. Leave this stitch on the needle. Next, bring the working yarn through the first stitch on the back needle as if to knit, and leave that stitch on the needle.

Step 1 Bring the working yarn through the first stitch on the front needle as if to knit, and slip that stitch off the needle.

Step 2 Bring the working yarn through the next stitch on the front needle as if to purl, and leave this stitch on the needle.

Note Here it gets a little tricky. When going from the front needle to the back needle, be sure that the working yarn does not end up over the front needle. This will become a yarn over, adding a stitch and a making a hole! The working yarn should come under the front needle and up between the two needles.

Step 3 Bring the working yarn through the first stitch on the back needle as if to purl, and slip that stitch off the needle.

Step 4 Bring the working yarn through the first stitch on the back needle as if to knit, and leave this stitch on the needle.

Repeat these four steps until you have one stitch remaining on each needle, and then follow steps 1 and 3.

instructions

Using the US #4 needles, cast on 64 stitches. Slip the stitches to the US #2 double-pointed needles and distribute evenly over the four needles. Join, being careful not to twist your stitches.

Work in stockinette stitch in the round (just knit) for 6" (15cm) from cast-on edge. (Use a locking stitch marker or the tail from the cast-on to let you know the beginning and end of the round.)

heel flap

Starting at your marker, knit 16 stitches from needle 1 and 1 stitch from needle 2 (17 sts). Turn, and slip the 16 stitches from needle 4 onto the needle with the 17 stitches (33 sts), which will now be needle 1. Needles 2 and 3 will not be used while working the heel flap; work back and forth on needle 1.

Note Slipping the first stitch on each row will make it easier to do the knit pick up along the side of the heel flap later on. All of your slip stitches will be as if to purl, so that you are not twisting the stitches, and with the yarn in back.

Row 1 (WS) Slip 1, purl to the end.

Row 2 (RS) Slip 1, * k1, slip 1*; repeat from * to * to end, end k2.

Row 3 Slip 1, purl to the end.

Row 4 Slip 1, k2, *slip 1, k1*; repeat from * to * to end.

Repeat these four rows until the heel flap measures 3" (7.5cm), ending with a purl row.

turning the heel

Note Count your stitches each time you have completed the purl (even-numbered) rows. The number of stitches before the gap on your right needle and the stitches remaining on your left needle should match.

Row 1 (RS) K18, slip 1, k1, psso, k1, turn.

Row 2 (WS) P5, p2tog, p1, turn.

Row 3 K6, slip 1, k1, psso, k1, turn.

Row 4 P7, p2tog, p1, turn.

Row 5 K8, slip 1, k1 psso, k1, turn.

Row 6 P9, p2tog, p1, turn.

Row 7 K10, slip 1, k1, psso, k1, turn.

Row 8 P11, p2tog, p1, turn.

Row 9 K12, slip 1, k1, psso, k1, turn.

Row 10 P13, p2tog, p1, turn.

Row 11 K14, slip1, k1, psso, k1, turn.

Row 12 P15, p2tog, p1, turn.

Row 13 K16, slip 1, k1, psso, k1, turn.

Row 14 P17, p2tog, p1, turn (19 sts).

gusset and foot

With an empty needle, knit 9 stitches of the heel. Knit the remaining 10 stitches onto a second empty needle. Using this same needle, knit pick up 18 stitches along the side of the heel.

Place the 18th stitch onto an empty needle, and with that same needle, knit the 15 stitches from needle 2 (16 sts).

With an empty needle, knit the 16 stitches of needle 3. Take an empty needle, and knit pick up 18 stitches along the side of the heel. Then knit the remaining 9 stitches from needle 4 onto that same needle.

You should have 27 stitches on needles 1 and 4 and 16 stitches on needles 2 and 3. Return to working in the round with all five needles.

gusset decrease

Rnd 1 Knit.

Rnd 2 On needle 1, knit to last 3 stitches, k2tog, k1. On needle 2, knit to end. On needle 3, knit to end. On needle 4, k1, slip 1, k1, psso, knit to end.

Repeat these 2 rounds until 64 stitches remain (16 stitches on all four needles). Knit even until foot measures 6" (15cm), or 2" (5cm) less than final length from base of heel to toes.

toe

Rnd 1 Knit.

Rnd 2 On needle 1, knit to last 3 stitches, k2tog, k1. On needle 2, k1, slip 1, k1, psso, knit to end of needle. On needle 3, knit to last 3 stitches, k2tog, k1. On needle 4, k1, slip 1, k1, psso, knit to end of needle.

Repeat these 2 rounds until 12 stitches remain (3 sts on each needle).

Using needle 4, knit the 3 stitches of needle 1 (6 stitches on needle 4). Slip the stitches from needle 2 onto needle 3 (6 stitches on needle 3).

finishing

With tapestry needle, graft stitches together using Kitchener stitch.

SIMPLE YARN SUBSTITUTION

If you fell in love with the Rolled Cuff Socks but you do not wish to dye the yarn, I found the perfect substitution yarn. It is KPPPM from Koigu Wool Designs, 100% wool. You will need 2 skeins, 1³/₄ oz (50g), 175 yds (160m) each. We were able to keep the same needle size and match the gauge. The sample swatch for the KPPPM yarn is knit up in color "121."

THE WOMEN OF KOIGU

On a cloudy September day, I arrived at Koigu Wool Designs in Williamsford, Ontario, Canada. It was here that I met the women of Koigu: Maie, Taiu, and Kersti Landra, three generations of women of Estonian descent. Maie and Taiu are mother and daughter and business partners; they are so close that they finish each other's sentences. Kersti is Taiu's daughter. The business of color, fiber, and design is so much a part of their lives, it is as commonplace to them as taking a breath.

Koigu started with 250 goslings, then goats, rabbits, flax, and finally sheep! A summer retreat turned into not just a home but a business. As we walked over to the farmhouse, Taiu told me that the bricks for the house had been made locally; they had a distinct orange color and are known as Chatsworth Bricks.

I looked around the kitchen, where the yarns were originally dyed, and saw the tables, the floor, and tree limbs in front of the house where the yarn hung to dry—this is where it all started. Today there is a sleek green building that houses the entire operation.

The name Koigu comes from Maie's late husband's family's former estate in Estonia. It honors a way of life that was lost when the Russians invaded Estonia. When Maie was eight years old, her family moved to Vancouver Island. They lived on a seed farm on the coast for two years. I can only imagine the visual impact this must have had on her. She spoke of the acres and acres of flowers in bloom, color everywhere.

The family moved to Toronto, where there is a large Estonian population.

Maie grew up in Toronto, with a longing for those idyllic days on Vancouver Island. In 1960, Maie graduated from art college and for the next twenty years painted in watercolor and egg tempera, selling her work through galleries.

In 1972, Koigu was purchased as a summer place, then in 1980 the family moved there full time. In the late 1970s, Maie began to do tapestries, and Koigu Wool began out of necessity—Maie was unable to find yarns in the colors she wanted for her weaving.

This is where the sheep come in. Maie thought she would raise the sheep, spin the yarn, dye the yarn, and then knit and weave with this yarn. Maie took spinning classes, and Taiu tagged along. Taiu immediately took to spinning and soon became proficient at it.

Maie began selling her one-of-a-kind garments at crafts fair, at her peak doing twelve to thirteen fairs a year. She and Taiu also started bringing some of the yarn with them, and people scooped it up. It quickly became apparent that they couldn't keep up with handspinning the fleece of 250 sheep.

Soon they began transporting the fleece to mills in Canada. As time went on this became impractical, and now Koigu yarns are custom spun to their specifications at large industrial mills, the fiber coming from the world market.

The first yarn Maie dyed and knitted with was a worsted weight yarn. Her customers were asking for a thinner, lighter weight yarn, something they could wear against their skin. Going through her stash, Maie found a lightweight Merino wool she had bought from a store that was going out

of business—this yarn was the precursor to KPM and KPPPM. When that stash was used up, Maie and Taiu found a mill that could make the same sort of yarn for them.

Today Koigu Wool employs three full-time and three part-time employees. They ship their yarn around the world, and have a cult following. As I toured the facility I could only imagine how great it must be to walk into this building on a bleak winter's day. Color was everywhere. The efficiency of the operation was also impressive.

The building was constructed in stages as the need for more space arose. We started at the back of the building, passing bales of undyed yarn to enter the drying rooms. The wettest yarn is placed in the first room, where cedar lines the walls and heat and fans are always on. As the yarns dry, they are moved to a second similar room—saunas for yarn!

Once the yarn has dried, it goes to Diana Brown. She takes the 500-gram skeins (eight at a time) and transforms

"Find a fiber you love and work with that."

THIS PAGE, CLOCKWISE FROM TOP LEFT: The first thing you see when you go up the driveway to Koigu is this beautiful barn. Rhichard Devrieze at work in the Rainbow Room; here he rinses newly dyed yarn. The sheep gather for a treat of apples. Maie Landra, whose hands are never still. Yarn just finished being made into 50 gram skeins. OPPOSITE PAGE: Taiu, Maie, and Kersti Landra and their dog, Jasmine.

THIS PAGE, CLOCKWISE FROM TOP LEFT: The wet room, where yarns are prepared for dyeing. Hand-dyed yarn, just out of the oven, cooling prior to rinsing. The women of Koigu heading home at the end of the day. Jasmine searches for frogs at the pond. Thistles are one of Maie's favorite flowers. Yarns out of the drying room waiting for Diana Brown to make them into 50 gram skeins. OPPOSITE PAGE, LEFT TO RIGHT: Chatsworth brick has a distinctive orange coloring. Koigu Painter's Palette Premium Merino (KPPPM) bursts from the shelf.

them into 50-gram skeins on a most impressive machine. Then the skeins go to the twisting station, where they are labeled and twisted, then off to the packing room to be shipped.

But I've left out the most important room—the Rainbow Room, so called by Maie, who prefers this name to Dye Room. "Rainbow" room it is—warm walls, lots of windows, the idea of color everywhere. They had just replaced the stoves and ovens, the new ones shiny, custom made, and ready for the job at hand. In the efficiently organized Rainbow Room, we found Rhichard Devrieze hard at work. Rhichard did a three-year apprenticeship at Koigu Wool Designs before he began to dye yarn on his own! I learned that he is a weaver, and he raises Merino sheep.

After watching Rhichard at work, we moved on to the showroom, and it was here we sat down to talk, surrounded by cubbies full of yarn. Maie's hands were never still, knitting away, as we talked. I asked her about this, and she quoted her mother, who said a woman's hands should never be idle.

Maie was trained as an artist, and it was very exciting for me to see her watercolors, egg tempera paintings, tapestries, and needlework. Maie sees color everywhere—not just the surface color, but what lies underneath. I think it is this color sense that makes her yarns so attractive. She is constantly exploring color and its interaction—the excitement of this process is why there are so many colorways in their yarns.

Later we walked the land, visiting the sheep and walking around the pond where her late husband, Harry, would swim every day in good weather. Though the farm is isolated, it never felt lonely to me—it was so full of life.

Maie, Taiu, and Rhichard dye the variegated yarns. They have found over the years that they prefer to work when it is quiet, so Richard will start his day at five in the morning, and Maie and Taiu will often work at night when all the employees have gone home and the phones stop ringing. Taiu also handles the business side of Koigu Wool Designs, answering phones, taking orders, and going to trade shows.

When I asked Maie and Taiu what advice would they give to someone dyeing yarn for the first time, here is what they said: "Learn as much as you can about the yarn, the fibers, the dyes, the equipment you might need. Find a fiber you love and work with that."

If you are thinking of starting a business dyeing yarn, they advise: "You need to have stick-to-it-ness; don't give up. It takes several years for a business to become viable." Maie also said that you will need to do more than just dye the yarn—you must also have pattern support.

Maie and Taiu told me that what keeps them going is the visual enjoyment, other people's appreciation of what they do, and a responsibility to the people who appreciate them.

resources

I would like to thank the many yarn suppliers who provided me with the yarns we used for the dyeing section of the book, as well as the yarns we suggest as alternate yarns for many of the patterns. All of the yarns used in this book are available from The Yarn Tree (www.theyarntree.com) and many local yarn shops.

I would also like to thank Lantern Moon for supplying the needles used in the photo on page 31.

Yarns We Dyed

Ashland Bay Trading Company, Inc.
PO Box 2613
Gig Harbor, WA 98335
253-851-6150
ashlandbay.com

Capistrano Fiber Arts Studio
31861 Via Montura
San Juan Capistrano, CA 92675
949-493-5951
CapFibArt@aol.com

Catalina Yarn
309 Fairmont Court
Saint Charles, IL 60175
888-900-9276
catalinayarns.com

The DMC Corporation
77 South Hackensack Avenue
Bldg. 10F
South Kearney, NJ 07032-4688
973-589-0606
www.dmc-usa.com

Frog Tree
PO Box 1119
East Dennis, MA
508-385-9476
frogtreeyarns.com

Green Mountain Spinnery
PO Box 568
Putney, VY 05346
802-387-4528
spinnery.com

HABU Textiles
135 West 29th Street
Suite 804
New York, NY 10001
212-239-3546
habutextiles.com

Hand Jive
3400 Arroyo Ave.
Davis, CA 95618
916-806-8063
handjiveknits.com

Henry's Attic
5 Mercury Ave.
Monroe, NY 10950
845-783-3930

Joseph Galler, Inc.
5 Mercury Ave.
Monroe, NY 10950
845-782-2548

Sweet Grass Wool
4528 US Hwy 12
Helena, MT 59601
888-222-1880
sweetgrasswool.com

Thirteen Mile Farm
13000 Springhill Road
Belgrade, MT 59714
406-388-4945
lambandwool.com

Treenway Silks
501 Musgrave Road
Salt Spring Island
British Columbia, Canada
V8K 1V5
250-653-2345
treenwaysilks.com

Treliske Organic Wools
2RD
Roxburgh
Central Otago
New Zealand
64-3-446 6828
treliskeorganic.com

Suggested Alternate Yarns

Chasing Rainbows Dyeworks
1700 Hilltop Drive
Willits, CA 95490
nancy.finn@sbcglobal.net

Harrisville Designs
PO Box 806
Harrisville, NH 03450
603-827-3333
harrisville.com

Koigu Wool Design
RR #1
Williamsford, Ontario, Canada
N0H 2V0
888-765-9665
koigu.com

The Schaefer Yarn Company Ltd.
3514 Kelly's Corners Road
Interlaken, NY 14847
800-367-9276
schaeferyarn.com

Beads

Toho Shoji
990 Sixth Ave.
New York, NY 10018
212-868-7465
tohoshoji-ny.com

Knitting Needles

Lantern Moon
7911 N.E. 33rd Drive, Suite 140
Portland, OR 97211
800-530-4170
lanternmoon.com

Tools

Skeining tool
The Yarn Tree
347 Bedford Avenue
Brooklyn, NY 11211
718-384-8030
theyarntree.com

Foam brushes, masking tape
Your local hardware store

Measuring cups, measuring spoons, digital scale, candy thermometer, metal muffin tin and timer
King Arthur Flour
800-827-6836
kingarthurflour.com/shop/

Taper tip syringe
Rupert, Gibbon & Spider/Jacquard Products
800-442-0455
jacquardproducts.com

Nitrile gloves
Lab Safety Supply
800-356-0783
LSS.com

Respiratory protection
Northern Safety Co., Inc.
800-631-1246
northernsafety.com

Dyes & Chemicals

Kool-Aid, food coloring, baking soda, distilled white vinegar, noniodized salt
Your local grocery store

Ashford Wool Dyes
In Canada
Treenway Silks
888-383-7455
treenwaysilks.com
In the United States
Foxglove Fiberarts Supply
877-369 4568
foxglovefiber.com
In New Zealand
Ashford Handicrafts Limited
64 3 308 9087
ashford.co.nz

Jacquard Acid Dyes, Procion MX Fiber Reactive Dyes, reduran, urea soda ash, Superclear, Synthrapol
Rupert, Gibbon & Spider/Jacquard Products
1 800 442-0455
jacquardproducts.com

PRO WashFast Acid Dyes, PRO One Shot Dyes, Kiton Acid Dyes, PRO Print Mix SH, PRO Dye Activator, citric acid
PRO Chemical & Dye
1 800 228-9393
prochemical.com

Gum tragacanth
Earthues
1 206 789-1065
earthues.com

further reading

Albright, Barbara, **The Natural Knitter: How to Choose, Use, and Knit Natural Fibers from Alpaca to Yak,** Potter Craft, 2007.

Bohmer, Harald, **Koekboya: Natural Dyes and Textiles, A Color Journey from Turkey to India and Beyond,** Kendi, 2002.

Delamare, Francois, and Guineau, Bernard, **Colors: The Story of Dyes and Pigments,** Harry N. Abrams, 2000.

Knudsen, Linda. **Synthetic Dyes for Natural Fibers,** Interweave Press, Inc., 1986.

Milner, Ann. **The Ashford Book of Dyeing,** Revised Edition, Shoal Bay Press, 1998.

Rex, Susan. **Dyeing Wool and Other Protein Fibers: An Introduction to Acid Dyes,** Susan Rex, 2004.

Square, Vicki, **The Knitter's Companion,** Interweave Press, Inc., 1996

Van Stralen, Trudi. **Indigo, Madder & Marigold:** A Portfolio of Colors from Natural Dyes, Interweave Press, Inc., 1993

Vogel, Lynn. **Twisted Sisters Sock Workbook: Dyeing, Painting, Spinning, Designing, Knitting,** Interweave Press, Inc., 2002.

acknowledgments

There are so many people to thank. A prominent politician once said that it takes a village to raise a child—well, it takes an entire community to write a book. First, I have to say thank you to Natalie Kaire; if not for her gentle prodding, I never would have written a book! I also have to thank her for introducing me to my agent, Joy Tutela. Joy understood me right from the beginning and has been my most important advocate.

Shawna Mullen, of Potter Craft, brought the idea of a dye book to the table and allowed me to soar with my vision.

A very special thank you goes to Julia Arnold—she entrusted me with her brand-new camera to take with me on my travels.

Another important person is Bob Grady, who dog-sat for Barley when I traveled for the book.

Eddie and Paul Lenoci, my landlords, for building my beautiful studio where I find peace and inspiration daily. Eddie also built the first prototype of my skeining tool from a rough sketch I had drawn.

Chick Sgroi for getting it when I showed up with a piece of PVC pipe, a block of wood, and a threaded rod and said, "I need a tool made just like this but in wood, and it has to be pretty."

Mitzi Good wore many hats during this project. She also took on the very important job of keeping me organized—no easy task!

Laura Altman and Shannon Brock for always being there and never letting the sky fall!

And to Darlene Hayes and Lori Lawson for taking time out of their very busy schedules to contribute patterns to the book, thank you!

Behind the scenes were many busy people, some playing dual and even triple roles!

From The Yarn Tree Community came all of the very talented people listed at right.

THE CODESIGNERS
Shannon Brock
Yvette Byas
Laura Cooper
Rachel DeNys
Donna Fiscina
Mitzi Good
Kimberly Kauffman

THE KNITTERS AND CROCHETERS
Laura Altman
Julia Arnold
Nancy Baugh
Shannon Brock
Yvette Byas
Caroline Byrne
Rachel DeNys
Erin Durnin
Mitzi Good
Angie Lendle
Tara Swanson

THE MODELS
Laura Altman
Erin Durnin
William Glenday
Mitzi Good
Natalie Kaire
Namiko Ketchie
Slade Koval
Toni Koval
Jackie Lora
Tara Swanson

acknowledgments *(continued)*

TECHNICAL EDITORS–DYE CHAPTERS

The following people reviewed the dye recipes for accuracy:

Vicki Jensen, PRO Chemical & Dye

Rowena Hart, Ashford Handicrafts, Ltd.

Noelle Faulkner and Sue Stover, Rupert, Gibbon &
Spider/Jacquard Products

TECHNICAL EDITOR–KNIT & CROCHET PATTERNS

Nancy Baugh

TECHNICAL ILLUSTRATORS

Elizabeth Asawa

Annie Rudden

PHOTOGRAPHERS

Donna Alberico–Fashion

Kristin Duvall–Still Life

PHOTOGRAPHER'S ASSISTANT AND STYLIST

Mitzi Good

PHOTO EDITOR

Mitzi Good

ASSET/FILE MANAGEMENT

Julia Arnold

Two local businesses were kind enough to allow me to shoot in and around their facilities. Khim's Millenium Market let us shoot Namiko in front of their shop very early one morning. Baci & Abbracci opened the restaurant's beautiful backyard garden so that we could spend the morning shooting the crochet shawl. If you are ever in my neighborhood and want to have a great meal, this is the place to go.

Most of all I want to say Thank You to the many people, customers, and students alike who have passed through the doors (both real and virtual) of The Yarn Tree—your support is so important to me!

And finally the staff of Potter Craft, for their hard work in making this into such a beautiful book.

index